BIG JACK

THE LIFE AND TIMES OF JACK CHARLTON

STAN LIVERSEDGE

First Published in the U.K. November 1994 by
The Publishing Corporation U.K. Ltd. of Haltgate House,
Hullbridge Road, South Woodham Ferrers,
Essex CM3 5NH. Tel & Fax: 0245 320462.
Marketing & Sales Tel: 081 993 1965 and 0850 698179.

TITLE:- BIG JACK.

ISBN:- 1 897780 81 8

SLEEVE - DESIGN BY:
JOE ELGIE

TYPESETTING BY:
SEXTON & COMPANY,
32 HERSCHELL ROAD, LEIGH-ON-SEA, ESSEX.
TEL & FAX: 0702 710617.

PRINTED IN ENGLAND BY:
CLAYS LTD, ST IVES PLC
BUNGAY, SUFFOLK.

Contents

FOREWORD

Big Jack... "Yer man"

When the World Cup of 1994 had come to its conclusion, three men in particular had left an indelible mark upon the competition, and none of them had been involved as players on the world stage. There was Diego Maradona, the swarthy, muscular Latin-American who was banished from the tournament in disgrace, just at a time when he was seemingly about to demonstrate that he could and would inspire Argentina to a place in the final, at least.

There was the Swiss referee with the almost unpronounceable name who, having given Manchester United cause for righteous indignation during their European Cup game against the Turkish side Galatasaray, made a decision which brought about defeat for Belgium, in their World Cup match against Germany in the United States. Germany won 3-2, and went through to the quarter-finals, while the referee afterwards admitted that he had been wrong in denying the Belgians their claim for a penalty. The referee paid the penalty for his error by being sent back to Switzerland, his World Cup at an end.

And then there was Jack Charlton, an Englishman in charge of a bunch of players drawn from just about everywhere in the British Isles. Big Jack, a World Cup winner as a player in 1966, a man who, according to report, had never been given the chance to manage the England International team, and who had then been able to extract some sort of sweet revenge by steering the Republic of Ireland to the finals in America, while England's players were left to reflect on what might have been.

There were those who claimed that if Alan Shearer had been fit at a time when his striking ability was sorely needed, England would have qualified. That may well be true.

And there were those who averred that had Big Jack Charlton been in charge of England's destiny, they would have gone to the World Cup finals, with or without the services of Alan Shearer. As things turned out, we shall never know.

What we do know is that Jack Charlton and his bunch of players did the Republic of Ireland proud, for the second time in a World Cup tournament, and that Jack himself (like Maradona and the Swiss referee) fell foul of the authorities. While Diego and the referee were expelled from the tournament, Jack was simply fined, but £10,000 isn't exactly chicken-feed, even if you can well afford to fork out that kind of cash.

Remarkably, when the verdict of FIFA became known (the Football Association of Ireland was fined a similar sum of money, while striker John Aldridge copped a £1,250 fine), the Irish fans showed exactly what they thought about the ruling body's decision; they dipped deeply into their own pockets and came up with more than enough cash to pay the lot.

In short time, the amount of money raised by collections and contributions soared to £100,000, and Big Jack and the Irish officials were overwhelmed. Jack pointed out that (a) the money raised couldn't be used to pay off the fines, in any case, and (b) he could afford to fork out the £10,000 himself. So, thanks very much, and the money raised by those wonderful fans could be donated to charity.

Jack Charlton has been described as "the honest hustler", and from personal knowledge of him, I always found him to be a straight talker. Not long after the 1966 World Cup, he and I got together to do a bit of business, and we concluded this business over a pint in a pub up on the Pennine moors, between Leeds and Oldham. Right through the time we were working together, we never had an argument, or even a cross word, though Big Jack, by his own admission, can be a bit of a cussed character!

His manager during his days as a Leeds United player, Don Revie, discovered that for himself. And during the 1994 World Cup in the United States there were occasions when Jack Charlton wasn't overpleased with the media. At one stage, he was talking to them in front of the television cameras, and he referred to them as "you lot." Yet he retained their respect.

I can remember one distinguished journalist finding himself without accommodation on one footballing trip, and Jack Charlton was the man who came to his rescue, giving him the chance to kip down on a room-sharing basis. The journalist never forgot the generous gesture and remained a Jack Charlton fan for all time.

There are some odd characters among the Pressmen of this world, and, being only human, they are apt to take offence if they feel they're being slighted or treated in cavalier fashion by so-called sports stars. Football managers, for instance, have sometimes paid for their high-handed attitude to the people striving to conduct interviews.

The late Sir Matt Busby was a past-master when it came to man-management. Players used to go into his office with thoughts of asking for a transfer, and they would come out having been charmed by "the boss" and almost wondering just why they'd gone in to see him in the first place.

Jack Charlton's style is different from that of Busby in many ways, but he is also good when it comes to managing players. Striker Tony Cascarino, whose contribution to the cause of the Republic of Ireland in the 1994 World Cup was brief, of necessity, (his main concern was trying to get over an injury) made it clear he wouldn't desert his manager or his team-mates when offered the chance to return home in advance of the main party.

A former Republic of Ireland player, Mick McCarthy, also gave Jack Charlton a tremendous vote of confidence. McCarthy, who had been the team's captain during the 1990 World Cup, became the team boss at Millwall, and he had this to say about Big Jack in the Summer of '94: "His secret is that the players trust him. He looks after his boys; he's very loyal." A sentiment which would surely have been echoed by Kevin Moran, to name but one.

When I first got to know him, Jack Charlton lived in a modest enough house in Leeds. Now he can afford something rather better, but he's never got above himself, as the saying goes. Whenever we met, just about the first thing he would say to me was: "Go on, give us a fag." Jack certainly enjoyed his smoke.

I used to wonder if I was the only one from whom he begged a cigarette, but I discovered that it was a habit he had. However, I finally got my own back when I met him at a sportsmen's dinner. Jack was the guest speaker that evening, and as we shook hands and started to chat before the function began, I got my piece in first.

"Before you ask me to give you a fag," I told him, grinning, "let me tell you that I can't, I gave up smoking several years ago. Sorry I can't oblige!"

I've seen it said that Jack was not cut out to be a club manager, and this despite the success he enjoyed: promotion with Middlesbrough and Sheffield Wednesday, and a Manager-of-the-Year award. However, it is true that during his time at Ayresome

Park, at Wednesday and at Newcastle United, the teams he managed were not exactly famed for their flair.

Workmanlike, yes; solid at the back, yes; seldom likely to excite, or to suffer defeat. I believe there's something to be said for the theory that a team often reflects its manager, and if the manager has been a defender, then the odds are that it will give little or nothing away at the back. By the same token, if a manager was famous for scoring goals during his playing career, then you will often find that his team is noted more for its attacking attitude than for its ability to prevent the goals going in.

Jack Charlton's teams at club level were sound defensively, if short on finesse. And it could never be denied that he did an effective job, even if he wanted his men to "play one-two's with God," as one soccer insider described it to me.

No matter whether it was at club or international level, Jack never had the slightest qualms about doing the job his way, and his way worked out well enough, even if sometimes the fans expressed their criticisms of the lack of style. As happened at Newcastle, Big Jack simply shrugged his shoulders and walked away. He "didn't need that kind of hassle."

When it comes to the Republic of Ireland, his fame has known no bounds. On the eve of the World Cup match against Holland, an Irish newspaper even published a special prayer for rain in Florida when the Republic met the Dutch in the steamy heat of Orlando!

Never mind that Big Jack was advised by a FIFA official to "stop moaning", even before he had been fined for what was termed "constant misbehaviour", in Irish eyes he could do no wrong. And Irish Prime Minister, Albert Reynolds, summed it up when, referring to Jack's favourite hobby, fishing, he made a point concerning the triumph over Italy in the initial group game: "Jack has been made a freeman of the city of Dublin and an honorary Irishman. What can we do after a performance like this?" And the Taoiseach supplied his own answer: "I suggest we make him Minister of Fisheries in the next Irish government."

Twenty-four hours after Ireland's defeat at the hands of Holland, Jack was answering questions about his intentions regarding the job of managing the Republic, and he reckoned he would give it a month in which to reflect, while saying also that he would almost certainly carry on until the 1996 European championships.

He mused on whether or not it was time for a change, time for fresh ideas, while suggesting he would stay if he were still wanted. Did he need to ask? Maybe, deep down, he felt he had taken the Republic as far as he could. And as he sat there in front of the television cameras, face reddened almost to the colour of a lobster by the hours spent out in the merciless sun, maybe he was thinking about the might-have-beens, not only with regard to the Republic, but with regard to the England job.

It has been said that when he did apply for that prestigious position, he didn't even receive the courtesy of a reply, and, knowing Jack, I doubt if he would take the job now, even if Terry Venables were to quit tomorrow and the FA came to him on bended knees.

Jack Charlton played for England under a World Cup-winning manager in Sir Alf Ramsey, and he played for Leeds United under a manager, Don Revie, who taught him so much about himself, as well as about the game. According to Peter Swales, the England job is "the hardest there is. It destroyed Don Revie; it didn't do Ron Greenwood much good; Bobby Robson didn't like it one bit, and Graham Taylor has had to live with it." Somehow, I reckon Jack Charlton could have handled it. After all, he has shown himself to be well capable of leading what could be termed a double life.

On the one hand, there is no more patriotic Englishman than Big Jack; on the other, he's a hero to the people of a nation whose relations with England have not been of the best, to say the least, through the past 25 years. So there indeed is a paradox.

Someone who knows Jack well sums up: "It's amazing. He can get off the plane in Dublin to a hero's welcome; they idolise him in Ireland. Then he can get off the plane again in Newcastle, which is more or less his home city, and he's treated almost with an air of indifference."

That latter observation may reflect attitudes since Big Jack was provoked by the fans into turning his back upon Newcastle United, the club he had supported as a lad, after having spent a brief spell as manager during the mid-1980's. Then, in 1986, he turned his attention to another kind of challenge: bringing international respectability to the Republic of Ireland's football team.

Yet he hasn't deserted his native North-East, even though he once lived in Leeds and now has a holiday bungalow on Ireland's west coast. Born in Ashington, Northumberland, on May 8th,

1935, the first of the four sons of Robert and Elizabeth Charlton, Jack is back in the area he calls home. And home now is a stone-built cottage at Stamfordham, a rural spot north of Newcastle.

The cottage comes complete with conservatory; there's a fairly long drive and there are a couple of houses nearby. The cottage may not be a mansion, but it is a place to which Jack can retreat from the glare of publicity which always attends his appearances as manager of the Republic of Ireland.

Like brother Bobby (now Sir Robert), Big Jack values his privacy. He married his wife, Pat, back in 1958, became the father of two sons and a daughter, and is now a grand-dad.

In various ways the Charlton brothers are alike; in others, different as cheese from chalk. Jack once thumped Bobby when they were kids, after Bobby had jocularly chided him about giving away a penalty and Bobby once couldn't contain his delight, after having got the better of big brother. "I've nutmegged you! I've nut-megged you!" he yelled.

While Bobby's recreation is golf, Jack's leisure pursuits are shooting, fishing and gardening. Jack fishes on a stretch of the River Tweed, up in the Border region, and his holiday bungalow in Ireland enables him to enjoy more fishing, on the River Moy's Ridge Pool, in County Mayo.

One of Jack's players, John Aldridge, who expressed his pleasure not only at being retained in the Irish squad for the first European-championship match in September, 1994, but at being chosen to play against Latvia in Riga (he scored twice in a 3-0 win), can thank his soccer boss, too, for having taught him something about the art of trout fishing, as well as football.

The game against Latvia was the 84th of Jack's reign as the Republic's manager, and he was prompted to observe: "I was pleased with the strikers. Aldo still has the knack of scoring goals." Aldridge was partnered by Niall Quinn, another with cause to be grateful to the manager.

Quinn was back on the international scene after having missed months of action, including the World Cup, because of an injury lay-off. He discovered "the boss" hadn't forgotten or discarded him. Jack can be a loyal man.

While Bobby Charlton's alma mater was Bedlington Grammar School, Jack attended Hirst Park School in Ashington. Whatever he learned there, he learned a lot more about life as he went along, and when it came to football, he had two of the best tutors in the business: Sir Alf Ramsey and Don Revie.

Big Jack never bothered to take elocution lessons, as Ramsey once did, but he did take the trouble to ask why Ramsey had picked him for England. And he once had the temerity to tell Ramsey he was talking "a load of crap." Having told Jack why he chose him: for his height, aerial ability, general mobility and tackling ability, Ramsey answered the "load of crap" charge by making it crystal-clear, in those clipped tones of his, that whatever Jack might think, things would continue to be done the way the manager decreed. Jack still thought the world of Alf Ramsey, as did the rest of the 1966 World Cup squad.

I would never pretend to have been a confidant of Jack Charlton, indeed, my dealings with him at close quarters were during the immediate, post-World Cup period, although our paths have crossed from time to time in more recent years. But through almost three decades, so far as I can judge, Jack doesn't seem to have changed in any way.

If he is well-off, he is also reputed to be careful with cash, and not just his own, but money belonging to others, such as the clubs he managed. While he did sign players, he didn't embark upon massive spending sprees when he was at Middlesbrough, Sheffield Wednesday or Newcastle. David Mills, the first footballer to be transferred for half a million pounds, reckoned that had Jack spent more lavishly, Boro' might well have done even better than they did (Charlton took them to promotion). Yet Mills thought enough of Jack to play for him twice.

To my knowledge, Jack can be capable of spontaneous generosity, as, for instance, when he decided, on the spur of the moment, to buy his parents a house. And at least one journalist, Jimmy Mossop, chief sportswriter on the Sunday Express, has publicly thanked Jack Charlton, after having been the recipient of a personal act of thoughtfulness.

Jimmy and I used to be friendly rivals while working in Manchester, and I'm told that even now, so many years on from when Jimmy became acquainted with Jack, they remain good buddies. The same can be said of Jack and a former footballing opponent, Maurice Setters, whom I knew as a player with Manchester United and Stoke City.

Jack recruited Maurice as his second-in-command at

Newcastle United and signed him on again as No.2 when he became manager of the Republic of Ireland. Maurice and Big Jack make a good pair; both were no-nonsense players at top level, and can present a somewhat formidable, pugnacious-jawed appearance calculated to demonstrate not only that they can be tough, when need be, but that they possess what football managers are fond of describing as "character." Certainly players, not to mention other folk, know where they stand with Big Jack, who, while being "the boss", is still capable of showing loyalty to those who serve him well.

Occasionally, Jack Charlton has been known to forget a name, or to come out with the wrong one - such as when he described centre-back Paul McGrath as John McGrath. Paul played a major role for the Republic on their way to and during the 1994 World Cup. John played at centre-half for Newcastle United many years past, and has managed clubs such as Bury, Preston North End and Halifax Town.

John McGrath is a witty, after-dinner speaker, and the story goes that as manager of hard-up Halifax, he faxed top clubs with the news that players were for sale, even the club cat. Tottenham Hotspur, it was reputed, responded in similar vein, with an offer for the cat.

Jack Charlton, too, can crack jokes when he's singing for his supper, as the saying goes, and he has proved himself to be a man of many parts. For instance, from 1977 to 1982, he was a member of that august body, the Sports Council, whose chairman, for a spell, was Sir John W. Smith, then also the chairman of Liverpool Football Club.

Jack is also at ease as a broadcaster or on TV. For my money, he appears to be more at home than brother Bobby, in front of the cameras, and he comes across well, even when he's doing nothing more exciting than a commercial. At the time of the 1994 World Cup, he could be seen extolling the virtues of a certain breakfast cereal, and if you were observant enough, you would have noticed in the background the figure of a woman. Jack's wife, Pat.

As a footballer with Leeds United, for whom he made 629 League appearances - a club record - Jack Charlton was appreciated by the Elland Road faithful to the extent that when his testimonial match was staged, no fewer than 34,000 people turned up. But in 1977, when he applied to become England's team manager, in a bid to succeed his former club boss, he got the thumbs-down.

Jack was to say later: "I was annoyed I wasn't even interviewed, and didn't even get a reply to the application I made." He believed he knew why: "I've got too many strong views, and tend to challenge accepted opinions." Well, England's loss has been the Republic of Ireland's gain.

Half an hour from Jack Charlton's Northumberland home stands the brooding Kielder Forest. A man can almost get lost inside it, and a 15-minute drive from the front door of Jack's cottage can see him fetch up at Newcastle airport and thus put him little more than two hours from Dublin, with its wide and busy O'Connell Street.

Jack has been realistic in his approach to the job of managing, and man-managing, at international level, and while the Republic's players know he's the boss, in turn, he lets them off the leash when the time is right. Together, they can share a laugh and a few drinks as they wind down, and Jack does enjoy his pint of Guinness and a drop of Irish whiskey.

He may be English to the core, but he also values his relationship with the Irish, whose Prime Minister was moved to say: "Jack's the man who has done for Ireland what none of us politicians could possibly achieve."

On the fringe of Dublin stands a pub with the odd name of Hill 16 (that's a reference to the uprising of 1916), and Jack and his players have been known to drop in and sink a pint or two there. Indeed, the pub is now regarded as Jack's local when he's in the Emerald Isle.

He's said he doesn't lay down hard-and-fast rules; it's a matter of people using their common sense. "The players can have a drink when I say they can. After games, I leave them to get on with what they want to do, as long as they behave themselves."

One of the things which endeared the Irish fans to Big Jack is the fact that they can enjoy a party without giving offence. "The Irish love to sing and play their music. They'll drink the place dry, but they always behave and are welcomed in every country in the world," he has said about them.

In turn, the Irish have taken Jack Charlton to their hearts. If brother Bobby had the OBE and the CBE before being knighted, Jack had the OBE. Bobby became an honorary fellow of Manchester Polytechnic and was awarded an honorary MA degree by Manchester University; Jack was made an honorary Irishman and a Freeman of the city of Dublin, and handed an honorary doctorate-of-science degree by Limerick University for his contribution to Irish sport. Ironically, from Ireland came the suggestion also that the English should make Jack a knight, like his brother.

In Ireland, they have a habit of referring to someone as "Yer man", and Jack Charlton, undoubtedly, has become *their* man. One of his declared principles has been never to outstay his welcome, though he has often said he would do the job as long as they wanted him.

By the time the 1996 European championships come round, Jack will be 61 years old and heading for his state pension in England. Whether or not his Republic of Ireland team will then be pitting its wits and its skills against the host nation remains to be seen.

This much is certain: his players will understand just what he wants from them because, as a coach and as a man-manager, he is an able communicator. When the need arises, he can call a spade a bloody shovel.

Should *you* feel tempted to communicate with Yer Man, the place to make contact is not Jack's home in the rural fastness of Northumberland, you should drop him a line, c/o the Football Association of the Republic of Ireland. The address: 8, Merrion Square, Dublin 2, Ireland.

Quotes

"The best thing that could happen to you would be for the club to leave you out; you're spoiling it for others, with that chip on your shoulder. You'd never do for me."

DON REVIE the player, giving Jack Charlton a piece of his mind.

"You should be playing for England, if only you would have the sense to do yourself and the club justice."

DON REVIE the manager, handing out another home truth to Jack Charlton.

"Looking back, I needed discipline."

JACK CHARLTON on himself.

"My mind was in a turmoil of emotions, and in the background was the thought of the seven deadly sins, of which pride is one. Somehow, I kept thinking that pride goeth before a fall, and yet, how could I help but be proud?"

CISSIE CHARLTON, talking after having seen her sons Jack and Bobby play their part in England's 1966 World Cup triumph.

"Yes, I know who you are: you're the boss."

POPE JOHN PAUL, at an audience in Rome with Jack Charlton and his Republic of Ireland players before the 1990 World Cup.

"A lot of Jack's players are happy to be picked for the Republic because they couldn't find a way to making it with England or Scotland."

BILLY BINGHAM, then the manager of Northern Ireland, on the eve of the crucial World Cup qualifier at Windsor Park, Belfast.

"What am I to do? Ignore a damn good player with Irish parents just because he happens to have been born in the UK?"

JACK CHARLTON, in reply to Billy Bingham.

"Calling us mercenaries is garbage. What Billy Bingham says is nothing short of scandalous; a disgrace. When I was first picked for Ireland, I didn't see pound notes before my eyes. I saw shamrocks. My pedigree is Irish, so is my patriotism, and it hurts whenever anyone questions it."

JOHN ALDRIDGE, rapping back at Billy Bingham's charge.

"We can't punish players who show dissent and let Jack Charlton get away with it; there is a basic standard of decorum we expect from managers and coaches."

FIFA spokesman **GUIDO TOGNONI.**

"One of my principles has been: never outstay your welcome. I have said many times that I would always do the job as long as they wanted me. I haven't seen any signs of them not wanting me, but before I ever fell out with them I would pack it in."

JACK CHARLTON, on his job as manager of the Republic of Ireland.

"We got a reputation for knocking the ball long. That always annoyed me, because we don't do that. We put it into areas of the field which cause defenders problems. It wasn't just a case of humping everything up there and hoping."

JACK CHARLTON, on the style of play he adopted for his team.

"I never want to fall out with the Irish people. I want to be able to enjoy the fishing and spend time at my bungalow with my friends over there for ever."

JACK CHARLTON

"If I were Mr Charlton, I would concentrate on Friday's game against Mexico and stop moaning. It's no coincidence that the only manager to complain is the one from Ireland."

FIFA General-Secretary **Sepp Blatter**.

"I think he (Jack Charlton) was a pain in the ass. He couldn't complain about being fined. He got his comeuppance, and when you look back at what the Republic of Ireland achieved, everything hinged on that one speculative kick by Ray Houghton which brought the winner against Italy. If that hadn't gone in, the Irish would have been catching the plane home."

PETER RHODES, former Football League referee.

"I don't know why Jack Charlton didn't get an interview - although I feel sure he would have been sent a reply to any application. There are a lot of things you can put right - with hindsight. I suppose he should have been given an interview."

PETER SWALES, former chairman of the England international committee.

"I want to apologise to Billy for what I said at the end of the game. I said a thing I will always regret. I'm very sorry I said it. It was in the heat of the moment. It was out of character."

JACK CHARLTON, after having made an abusive remark to the then team manager of Northern Ireland, Billy Bingham.

"The refereeing has been awful. It is the worst I have ever seen, and FIFA must take the blame. The referees are performing like robots, doing exactly what they are told, otherwise they know they will be on the next plane home."

Former FIFA Referee Clive Thomas on the 1991 World Cup.

"The England job is the hardest there is. It destroyed Don Revie; it didn't do Ron Greenwood much good; Bobby Robson didn't like it one bit; and Graham Taylor has had to live with it."

PETER SWALES, former chairman of the England international committee.

"Jack Charlton once laughingly observed about Bob Stokoe - who also hates being on the losing end - 'He'd fight you for the lemons at half time!'"

BOB PAISLEY, former Liverpool manager.

Mother's Pride

During the course of a long and varied career as a journalist, I have covered many major events, attended some top-table functions and reported on some big stories. For instance, in my days as a news reporter, I covered a royal visit and stood as close to the Royal family as it was possible to get. And in an era when the death penalty was still in existence for those who had committed the crime of murder, I sat inside a courtroom, the doors to which were then locked, while the judge returned to put on the black cap and pronounce sentence of hanging upon a woman who had buried her victim under a pile of coal.

In sport, I covered the finals of the World Cup, during which Brazil, and Pélé in particular, were alleged to have been kicked out of the competition by opposing teams. I got the chance to talk to some of the most famous people in soccer and in cricket, while I also interviewed some of the most illustrious names in showbiz.

I bought Violet Carson (Ena Sharples of Coronation Street fame) a gin and tonic in the bar of a theatre close by the Granada television studios in Manchester. I talked to Eric Morecambe and Ernie Wise, to Les Dawson and Jimmy Tarbuck, and I drove across to a place called Knotty Ash (yes, it does exist), on Merseyside, to beard Ken Dodd in his home there. Doddy was sufficiently tickled to see me that he called in script-writer Eddie Braben, and between them, they knocked out an hilarious piece of nonsense which I turned into an article for a brochure by the players of Liverpool Football Club.

In cricket, I ghosted articles by Clive Lloyd, captain of the West Indies team, and got to know Test wicket-keeper batsman Farokh Engineer, Lancashire captain Jack Bond and team-mates such as David Lloyd, David Hughes and Jack Simmons in the days when they were collecting trophies in the one-day Cup competitions.

When it came to football, I got to know some of the biggest names in the game: Sir Matt Busby, Bill Shankly, Bob Paisley, Joe Fagan, Kenny Dalglish, Ron Saunders, Harry Gregg, Alex Stepney,

Lou Macari, Joe Jordan, Sammy McIlroy, Joe Royle, Jack Charlton, AND I met a lady called Elizabeth, whom everybody knew simply as Cissie. She was the mother of the Charlton brothers: Jack, Bobby, Gordon and Tommy (yes, there were four of them).

One morning I was awake bright and early, ready to drive up to the Northumberland mining village of Ashington, just under 20 miles from Newcastle. I was going to see Mrs Cissie Charlton at her home in Beatrice Street, and my 250-mile round trip proved to be worth every moment of the time and trouble I had taken. I came face to face with a smiling, wavy-haired, bespectacled woman who most certainly did not put on airs and graces just because two of her lads had achieved fame as footballers.

I was there to interview Cissie Charlton not just about Jack and Bobby, but about herself, and she provided me with ample reward as she answered some searching questions with forthright candour during the several hours of our conversation. Among other things, as I nosey-parkered, I soon realised that Jack Charlton, with his no-nonsense, direct approach to things, was a real chip off the old block.

As for Cissie, she reminded me of an old aunt of mine who had also had a hard time of it when she was younger and who, as she passed middle age, still lived in a two-up, two-down cottage which had just one cold-water tap in the kitchen and an outside "privy." Since it was a communal backyard for about half a dozen cottages, all your neighbours knew when you needed to pay a visit to the toilet.

In spite of all the hard times, my aunt used to get up very early in the morning, then walk several miles to do a cleaning job in someone else's home. She lived to be 104 years old, and while Cissie Charlton was in her mid-50s when I met her, by the mid-1990's she was still going strong, at 82.

Like my old aunt, she lived in a two-up, two-down cottage with a backyard and, again like my aunt, she had gone out to work when she was in her early teens - in fact, she went "into service", as they used to say, travelling all the way to London from Ashington when she was but 14 years of age. Somehow, they don't seem to make them like my aunt and Cissie Charlton any more, and to talk to Cissie was not only an education, but a privilege and a pleasure. Here was a woman who had truly known what it was like to try to make ends meet, yet she had managed to keep on smiling.

Three years after having left the North-East for England's capital city, she was on her way home again, because her mother had been taken ill. Had she remained in London, the course of England's World Cup history might well have been altered; would the Charlton brothers still have played in the final of 1966?

As it was, Cissie went back to her native heath and, in due time, she got married to a miner. Her husband was earning just thirty shillings a week in the old currency, and after they had paid the licence fee for their registry-office wedding, they were left with thirteen shillings.

They didn't have what the old song referred to as "a stylish marriage", either, they simply caught a bus to get down to the registry office, and on their wedding night they were treated to a "posh" meal by one of Cissie's four brothers, George. You didn't have a honeymoon; you had what they called a housewarming, then it was straight back to work for the husband, which meant a seven-hour shift down the pit.

There came a time, however, when Cissie's husband, his health impaired after all his years as a miner, had to switch to a less-demanding job, and so his pay packet was that much lighter. Later on, he found himself redundant. But, of course, there was a bright side to the lives of Mr and Mrs Charlton, and, naturally, it wasn't long before Cissie got around to talking football, with special reference to her two eldest sons, Jack and Bobby.

Anyone who has ever talked to Cissie Charlton about soccer, as I did, would soon come to the conclusion that she knows considerably more about this game than some of the people who are in it. In fact, Cissie Charlton used to play football herself.

Up in the North-East, there was a footballer called Len Shackleton, and he was dubbed the Clown Prince of Football. He once wrote a book in which he included a chapter about directors. It caused a sensation at the time. The chapter was headed "What the Average Director Knows About Football" - and there followed a blank page.

Now THAT kind of commentary certainly couldn't apply in the case of Cissie Charlton, because she came from a family which was steeped in football. There's an old saying up in Cissie's part of the world that if you shout down a pit (not that there are many of them left, these days) up will pop a footballer.

Well, Cissie Charlton's husband may have been an exception, he was a miner, but he wasn't a footballer, or even a football nut. Cissie, however, had two sisters: Esther and Gladys, and four brothers: Jack, George, Stan and Jimmy, and the whole lot of them were weaned on football.

Cissie's father was called John Thomas Milburn (everyone soon shortened that to Tanner), and he was a goalkeeper. He went to some pains to ensure that his four sons and three daughters became proficient at sport, too. The girls even played soccer, and they shared the same changing quarters as their brothers.

All this I learned, as Cissie Charlton and I sat and talked in that modest pitman's cottage in Ashington, and she told me, with a twinkle in her eye: "Woe betide us if we returned home from an athletics competition without a wee trophy to show for our efforts."

As for her four brothers, they followed in their father's footsteps, because they all became professional footballers. So, with a family background like that, the odds were always that if Cissie ever had sons, one or two of them would inherit the footballing talent and make a living from the game, as her four brothers had done.

Each of them, like Jack Charlton originally started out, played at full-back, and three of the brothers: Jack, George and Jimmy, wore the colours of Leeds United, while Stan, the odd one out, as it were, saw service with three clubs: Chesterfield, Leicester City and Rochdale. Jack and Jimmy also played for other clubs, the former for Bradford City, the latter for Bradford Park Avenue, while George, like Stan, did a stint with Chesterfield.

When the brothers were kids, their Dad, Tanner, was their trainer, and their sporting activities were not solely confined to soccer. Cissie Charlton told me how the lads ran in handicap races, while in her own case, as well as playing football, she became captain of the school netball team. Right through her days of growing up, however, she retained her love for football, and when she married she nourished hopes that one day she would have sons and that like her four brothers, they would turn out to be footballers.

Jack and Bobby more than fulfilled Cissie's ambitions, while Gordon did follow Jack to Elland Road and spent six months there, having trials with Leeds United. In the end, however, he opted for a return to the North-East, where he spent some of his spare time playing football for a non-League club, Gateshead. As for a proper job, he qualified as an engineer in the Merchant Navy.

The fourth brother, Tommy, took after his Dad, who couldn't be termed a football fanatic but who enjoyed other sports, notably fishing and clay-pigeon shooting. Today, of course, in addition to his soccer fame, Jack Charlton is known as a fishing enthusiast, so maybe in that respect he, too, took after his father. Naturally, though, when the day dawned that Jack had to decide whether or not to follow his Dad down the pit or to take his chance as a young soccer hopeful, it was virtually no contest, and Cissie Charlton was the guiding light even if, deep down, she really believed that younger-brother Bobby was the one who would become a headliner in the game.

When I talked to Cissie, we went back to the boys' childhood, and I learned that Jack , "he's the fiery one in the family", could get into mischief as easily as the next one. Team-mate Norman Hunter was later to confirm that Jack "doesn't like being told what to do; he needed someone to get hold of him." Don Revie was the man who did that at Leeds, though it remains clear that even today Big Jack still doesn't like anyone telling him what to do.

It's not difficult to imagine Jack Charlton getting some good hidings when he was a nipper; there was an occasion when he and some pals raided the garden of a neighbour. The kids took with them a bag of sugar, pulled up sticks of rhubarb from the neighbour's garden, then doused them in the sugar and ate them. Another time, young Jack the lad sold a cauliflower to a woman, who then found out that the cauliflower had come from her own garden.

Cissie Charlton recalled incidents such as these and others, such as the time Jack and a friend turned up at a local garage and did something which aroused the ire of the garage manager, who retaliated by turning an oil hose on the pair of them. Jack's Mum wasn't best pleased when he turned up at home with his fair hair covered in oil.

Young Bobby Charlton was a different kettle of fish: where Jack was adventurous and, at times, went where others feared to tread, "wor kid" was shy to the extent that he would try to hide behind his mother's skirts when she was chatting to someone. When he did get himself into trouble, he would do a vanishing act, by nipping upstairs and getting into bed.

When we talked about football, Cissie Charlton indicated to me that while she had always believed Bobby would make it to the highest level of the game, she was nowhere near as certain that his big brother would be up there with him. Unlike "wor Bobby', Jack never clicked for schoolboy honours, and yet, when the World Cup final of 1966 had ended, and England had carried off the trophy by virtue of their extra-time victory over West Germany, Cissie rated her eldest son the top player in the tournament.

Coming from her, that was praise indeed, and, by the same token, while she gave way to no-one when it came to extolling the skills of Bobby, she wasn't blind, either. In fact, he came in for his fair share of criticisms. For instance, she reckoned that Bobby played a deep-lying role too often; she felt he should get further forward and use his famed shooting power even more than he did.

By the time I met her, Bobby was plying his trade with England and Manchester United, but that didn't prevent Cissie Charlton from telling me: "He hasn't the natural talent he showed when he was 15, and I think he should score more goals than he does." She did agree that he hadn't done badly, at that.

She recalled one game in which he played as a youngster, it was against the Welsh schoolboy side, and he demonstrated his shooting power with a drive which homed in on the target. On this occasion, however, Bobby didn't celebrate a goal - he came in for a telling-off, because the young Welsh 'keeper took the full force of the shot in the midriff, and as he bent double with the pain, the lad's mother gave vent to her feelings in no uncertain manner, despite an assurance from Cissie Charlton that he would recover very quickly, since he had only been winded.

When Manchester United made their move for young Bobby, it was make-up-your-mind time in the Charlton household, and Bobby's father was content to rely upon Cissie's sound judgment when it came to decisions involving soccer. So the teenager embarked upon a footballing career some 150 miles away from his native heath, and Cissie Charlton received a letter from a man living in the Manchester area chiding her for allowing the lad to leave home at such a tender age.

The writer also reckoned that Bobby Charlton should have been allowed to join another United, Newcastle United, instead of Manchester United, although (had he known it) Newcastle were Jack's favourites, while Bobby was a Sunderland supporter. Cissie Charlton didn't write back to tell the man to mind his own business, but she did send him a Christmas card.

There was an occasion when brother Jack received a letter from a football fan, too. It came from Barnsley, and arrived just at the time when he had been chosen to play for England against Scotland. There was no signature, but the message was far from complimentary. Instead of offering congratulations, the writer decried Jack's merits as a centre-half and said he (or she) couldn't comprehend how he had come to be selected for his country.

When Jack mentioned the matter to another England newcomer, Nobby Stiles, he learned that the Manchester United player had received a similar missive.

Not surprisingly, the vast majority of the fan mail both Jack and Bobby Charlton received was complimentary, and whenever they returned home to Ashington, Cissie Charlton was apt to produce a bundle of autograph books which were waiting to be signed by the pair of them.

Mrs Charlton struck me as a down-to-earth person who could recognise the faults in her offspring, even while she naturally, and justifiably, felt pride in their achievements. At the back of her mind, it seemed, was the fear of showing too much pride, in case it was followed by a fall. As she said after England's World Cup triumph, when interviewed by David Coleman on television: "I don't think any woman should have as much pride as I have, at this moment - it doesn't seem right."

She told me how, as a guest of the Football Association, she watched two of her sons playing in that dramatic final, and she kept telling herself that "this can't be real. I was such an ordinary Mum, the wife of a miner, living in a two-up, two-down cottage in a little Northumberland village. An ordinary Mum - more ordinary than many of the people who sat around me."

Yet, having witnessed the success her sons had achieved in football, she recognised also that other mothers could experience similar feelings of pride in what their own children made of themselves. And she recalled: "When the game ended, I saw Jackie run to Bobby and put his arm around his kid brother's shoulder. Bobby, I could tell, was too emotionally involved to speak. The television cameras captured the tears which he fought so hard to control."

It was an emotional time for Cissie Charlton, too. She met the rich and the famous: Harold Wilson, who was then the Prime Minister, Sir Stanley Rous, the president of FIFA, Lord Harewood, the president of Leeds United, and she and her husband had

7

enjoyed the pre-match hospitality of the Football Association as the players' families were taken to see a London show on the eve of the game.

At the reception after the final, Harold Wilson told Cissie Charlton about the time he had travelled up to Ashington, job-hunting, and when she talked to players from other countries, she commiserated with the Portuguese who, like the West Germans, were there. England had beaten Portugal in their semi-final, and Cissie Charlton felt that Eusebio and his team-mates were second-best only to the England lads, out of all the teams which had contested the finals. As she told me later: "England versus Portugal - that should have been the final."

It was Bobby Charlton who introduced Uwe Seeler, the West German captain, to Cissie, and he told her that "we feel no disgrace in having been beaten today. It was a fine game, and we need not be ashamed." A verdict with which Mrs Charlton agreed, even if she did have a soft spot for Portugal.

At the time I met her, Cissie and her husband had been married for more than 30 years, yet the furthest they had ever been on holiday was the Isle of Man. If the success of her footballing sons made her proud, it certainly didn't make her envious, and I felt that here was a wise woman. As she told me: "Life has been good to us."

She also said that she had learned "one golden rule: keep your nose out of your children's business when they grow up. They won't thank you for interfering, they will thank you for not." So far as I know, that remained her motto through later years, although there came a day in the Summer of 1994 when, once again, the views of Mrs Cissie Charlton were being canvassed.

By that time she was 82 years old, and while big brother Jack was making headline news as manager of the Republic of Ireland team in the World Cup finals in the United States, "wor Bobby" had just had a knighthood conferred upon him. Bobby, aged 56, declared that "this is the best thing that has ever happened to me - better than winning the World Cup."

It brought to mind the occasion when his one-time manager, Matt Busby, had been honoured in similar fashion and I had asked him: "What do I call you now?" To which the Manchester United team boss replied: "Call me what you've always called me." So I continued to call him "Matt."

Bobby Charlton's reaction to his own knighthood was similar. "I've always been Bobby; I expect my friends will still call me that." And Jack, who was with his team in Florida when the news broke, expressed his own pleasure at the accolade bestowed upon Bobby. Meanwhile, the brothers' mother, who was recovering from a fall which had left her with cracked and bruised ribs, toasted both her sons with a Guinness as she said: "I'm so proud of them."

And of her second-eldest son she said: "Our Bobby truly deserves this, because he has worked so hard all his life. I can hardly believe it: one lad leading his team into the World Cup and the other with a knighthood."

Mention of Cissie Charlton then brought back the memory of my own trip to Ashington to see her and talk to her, close on 30 years previously, and when we met I was left with the feeling that while she did indeed think a great deal of all her sons, perhaps Bobby was the one who was closest to her heart.

In the Summer of 1994, as she celebrated Bobby's knighthood, it was Jack Charlton who confirmed the impression I had got all those years ago, when he said: "Our mother will be proud of her lad. She's as well known in her own right as we are. Bobby has always been her favourite. She will be delighted for him."

Of course, she was - and I have to say, that whether or not Bobby was her favourite son, Big Jack never showed any sign of jealousy or resentment, to my knowledge. As he admitted, he and "wor kid" didn't always agree, but each of the brothers got on with his own life and, at the same time, maintained a good relationship.

I can recall going to a function near Liverpool at which Jack was the main speaker, and as he stood up he mentioned that Bobby had had to go to London on business that day, but he hoped to be able to get to the function, at some stage or other. Sure enough, Bobby Charlton did appear, having taken time and trouble, to give his big brother support, even after a busy and tiring day himself.

When I sat talking to Cissie Charlton in her home that day long ago, she was just grateful for the fact that she had been able to see her lads making good as footballers. As she told the then Prime Minister, Harold Wilson, when they were chatting after the 1966 World Cup victory: "If I could, I would have had eleven sons, and they would all have played for England!"

Even when the lads were growing up, however, Cissie and her

husband had no idea just how famous Jack and Bobby were to become. They never visualised the day dawning, for instance, when Ashington would honour the pair of them with a civic reception attended by thousands as the lads drove in an open car from that cottage in Beatrice Street to the council chambers.

Jack and Bobby were each presented with a tankard and a gold watch, then they moved on to yet another reception, one which had been organised by the local mineworkers' federation, and this time there was a silver tea service apiece. The people in the North-East are canny folk: they work hard, they play hard, and they're generous, especially to their own.

There was indeed one example of generosity still to come, and on this occasion it was a gesture from Jack Charlton to the parents who had lived their married lives in a two-up, two-down. Jack had been asked if he would open a show-house on a local housing estate, and when he went along to do the honours, he surprised himself, as well as his folks, by deciding, on the spur of the moment, that he would buy one of the new houses for them.

It was a semi-detached house, it cost £2,700, and Cissie Charlton and her husband were given no chance to say "Thanks, but no thanks." Jack reckoned that if he made the offer in front of witnesses, there was no way his parents could refuse. And so they accepted the offer in the spirit in which it was made and moved in.

Rocky Road To Fame

Fate has been kind, even bountiful, to the footballing brothers Charlton, though it's fair to say that neither Jack nor Bobby would ever come first in a beauty contest. Each has wisps of hair crossing a balding pate, each has a strong jaw-line and a somewhat jutting chin which gives the pair of them the kind of look that says you cross swords with them at your peril.

Taking them both together, you have to admit that for a couple of lads whose home was a two-up-two-down pitman's cottage, they haven't done too badly for themselves. Naturally, their mother, Cissie, was proud of them both, and she said as much, just as she had expressed her pride in them to me when we talked in her Ashington home shortly after they had won World Cup medals in 1966, as members of Alf Ramsey's England team. I got the impression then that Cissie Charlton always felt that Jack, the eldest of four brothers, could look after himself, and, of course, he has shown time and again through the years that he's extremely capable of doing so.

At times he's been a bit of a rebel, even an awkward cuss, as he once admitted to me. At times he's been irascible, fallen foul of footballing authority, as a player, as well as since he became a manager. At times he's harangued the media and referred to them with a number of adjectives. But if Jack Charlton has virtually challenged people to take him on, with that direct stare of his, he has never commanded less than respect, even if you might at times have found it difficult to love him. Big Jack is his own man and he goes his own way. If you don't like it, then it seems you'll have to lump it.

Anyone who knows anything about the Charlton brothers will know that they come from a family of footballers. So it's hardly surprising that Jack and Bobby have graduated to star status, although the two youngest of the four brothers certainly didn't follow in their footsteps. After Jack and Bobby came Gordon and Tommy. Gordon went into the Merchant Navy, while Tommy served an apprenticeship down the pit, and showed little or no interest in football.

Cissie Charlton's husband was a pitman, and Jack Charlton could so easily have become one, too. In fact, at one time during his early teens it seemed that it would become a straight choice of a career in mining or joining the police force. Big Jack was a six-footer, even in those days. He stood six feet two inches tall in his stockinged feet, and he took to the notion of becoming a policeman.

At the same time, while he put in his application to become a police cadet, he wanted another string to his bow, just in case. It seems that he was a canny lad then, and he's certainly confirmed this impression over the passing years. So Jack Charlton began a six-month training course at the same colliery where his father worked, and the idea was that when the six months were up, he would begin an apprenticeship by going down the pit.

As I said, there's that old saying in the North-East of England that if you shout down a mine shaft, up will come a footballer, but as it turned out, nobody needed to shout down a mine shaft for Jack Charlton to appear, because he never went down the pit, anyway. Instead, he became a professional footballer, thanks to what he regarded as his sideline.

In those early days, he regarded himself as a full-back, and he played for the local YMCA side. The ground on which the team played belonged to an engineering firm, and it was there that Jack was spotted by a scout from a club called Leeds United, which, in a manner of speaking, was a disappointment in itself, because Jack was a committed supporter of Newcastle United (a club he was later to manage).

Leeds United then were not exactly setting the footballing world on fire, even though they had a famous name as their manager. He was the man everyone called "The Major" - Major Frank Buckley, who had achieved fame and made headline news when he was the team boss of Wolverhampton Wanderers. It was there that he became noted as a pioneer of what was termed "the monkey-gland treatment", in an effort to improve the health and the all-round ability of professional footballers.

When the Leeds United scout appeared at the door of the Charlton residence, it was to suggest that Jack went down to Elland Road for a trial. At that stage, the lanky teenager was still waiting to hear from the police about his application to become a cadet, but that didn't prevent him from deciding to give football a go.

Jack's father was content to let the scout do the talking and Cissie Charlton to make the decisions, when it came to football, after all, she had played soccer herself. The verdict was that it couldn't do young Jack any harm, going down to Leeds, so it was arranged that he would let United's backroom staff take a look at him and put him through his paces.

Jack's parents accompanied him on the journey down to Elland Road, and they watched him take part in the trial game, which was held on a Saturday and which, as it turned out, was played in terrible conditions, because a blizzard was raging. Jack turned out in what was then his usual position - left-back - and he got through the game without mishap, despite the whirling snow which swept around the young hopefuls.

His performance was good enough for Leeds United to decide that they would offer him a contract. He was 15 years of age, he had just come to the end of his six-month training course at the colliery, and he still hadn't heard a dickey-bird from the police. So far as he was concerned, football offered a new challenge, and it was one he felt sure he would enjoy, after all, he was going to be paid for the pleasure of kicking a ball around, and that had to be an improvement on going down the pit, or putting on a uniform.

The Charltons returned to Ashington, and on the Sunday, Jack packed his gear, ready to go back to Leeds the following day and into digs there. All of a sudden, he was going to be a professional footballer and, he hoped, go right to the top. It was time to forget about an interview for the police force at Morpeth.

The Monday should have been the day when he kicked off with his mining apprenticeship; it also turned out to be the day that news came through from the police to say that his application to become a cadet had been successful. However, a twist of fate had decreed otherwise: Jack Charlton no longer wanted to become a copper; he had decided to concentrate on soccer.

From then on, the path to footballing fame turned out to be somewhat tortuous, and as he trod the rocky road, Jack Charlton saw managers come and go with some rapidity at Elland Road. After "The Major" there were Raich Carter, Bill Lambton and Jack Taylor, and after them, it was the turn of Don Revie to try his luck in the hot seat.

Raich Carter, of course, was a man whose name had become a household word when he was parading his talents as a player at club and international level, and when Leeds appointed this silver-haired hero, they were clearly hoping that some of his fame would rub off on to them. However, the time came when Carter departed, and first Lambton, then Taylor, got the opportunity to shine. Neither man was exactly famous in the Carter mould, and neither man stayed the course.

Jack Charlton almost didn't stay the course either. For one thing, he didn't see eye to eye with Don Revie. For another thing, he didn't feel he was making the kind of progress he should have done, indeed, it seemed to Jack that he wasn't getting anywhere at all. And this was largely because another character stood in his way. That character went by the name of John Charles.

With the passing months, Leeds United had decided that Jack Charlton would probably make a better centre-half than a left-back, so they switched him to the heart of the defence, as he graduated to reserve-team football. However, while he did manage to make the breakthrough to the senior side, he could never regard himself as an automatic choice, or even a regular, because Leeds always had the great John Charles.

This Welsh international, known throughout football as "The Gentle Giant", could play with equal aplomb at centre-half or centre-forward. If Leeds needed goals, they could rely upon Charles to score them; if the defence required shoring up, Charles was the man on whom they depended to do the job. It meant that for Jack Charlton, this was a most frustrating period.

It was around this time that Jack, as he admitted to me himself, began to have what today people call "an attitude problem." It was a problem which caused the aspiring first-teamer to start losing belief in himself, and the problem was compounded by the fact that some 50 miles away in Manchester, Jack's kid brother, "Wor Bobby", was beginning to command genuine attention as a potential star at Old Trafford.

John Charles had a brother, too. His name was Mel, and he became a Welsh international. He also left his native land to join Arsenal for the massive transfer fee of £45,000. Mel Charles, who played at centre-half, never quite achieved the star status of brother John, and possibly he suffered in the way that Jack Charlton felt he was suffering.

Slowly but surely, Jack was coming round to the way of thinking that he was never going to make his mark at Leeds United, and

14

that a parting of the ways appeared to be the best solution to the problem. Certainly, he never envisaged that he would stay at Elland Road long enough - a span of two decades - to become the club's record-holder when it came to League appearances: no fewer than 629, between 1953 and 1973. Not to mention a career with England which saw him claiming the ultimate trophy.

April 1957 was a significant month in the life of Jack Charlton. It was then that the predatory Italians demonstrated that money was virtually no object when it came to landing a footballer they coveted. In the case of Juventus, the footballer they coveted was "The Gentle Giant", and, while it might seem laughable now, when we scarcely blink as we talk about £3M transfer fees, the sum of money they were prepared to shell out for John Charles was regarded almost as outrageous. All of £65,000!

No matter that Leeds United did NOT want to lose their star player; no matter that the Leeds United supporters made it abundantly clear that THEY did not favour the deal; when the chips were down and the crunch came, the club decided there was no way it could reject an offer of £65,000. So that was the way in which, to coin a phrase or use a cliché, the cookie crumbled. John Charles was on HIS way to the land of the lira, and Jack Charlton benefitted from the crumbs.

It's interesting to see just how much of a reward John Charles received as his share of the transaction which made headline news at the time: according to report, Juventus were willing to part with another £10,000, which would go to "The Gentle Giant." So Big John went to Italy and became a much-loved star all over again, while Big Jack stayed at Leeds United and still simmered as he felt that very little had changed.

The departure of John Charles certainly did little to restore the fortunes of the Elland Road club, despite the money they had received for him from Juventus. Charles had gone, Leeds had cashed in, but results went from bad to worse, and at the end of season 1959-60, Leeds United went down to the Second Division, in company with Luton Town. Naturally, the fans of the Elland Road club expressed their displeasure, and even worse, Leeds United didn't give their supporters much hope about the future.

Far from showing that they had the will and the ability to bounce straight back to the First Division, Leeds laboured and lagged to such an extent that relegation to the Third Division began to look very much on the cards. As for Jack Charlton, he was feeling just as sorry for himself as he was for the club and its supporters. As he said later to me: "I felt that if Leeds were struggling so much, what hope was there for me?"

Later, Jack was to admit that a fellow called Don Revie, backed up by people such as Syd Owen, Les Cocker and Maurice Lindley, helped to turn him into an England international, though not before Revie had said a few unkind words to him, nor before Jack himself had offered to "take his coat off" to Syd Owen, after what could be termed a shouting match.

At a time when Revie was a team-mate, Jack Charlton was to hear him say: "The best thing that could happen to you would be for the club to leave you out; you're spoiling it for others with that chip on your shoulder." And a final, cutting sentence: "You'd never do for me." In the final analysis, of course, Jack DID "do" for Revie, to the extent that the Leeds United manager was telling his centre-half: "You should be playing for England."

But while Big Jack was going through what could be termed his "awkward phase" at Elland Road, the future appeared to be anything but rosy, and he was in such a dark mood that he finally decided to ask the club for a transfer. As for Leeds, at that time they didn't exactly do their utmost to talk him out of it.

So speculation mounted that Jack Charlton and Leeds would be parting company, and then the newspapers began to carry stories indicating that Liverpool, managed by Bill Shankly, were keeping a close watch on developments. Jack himself began to ponder on a future which included playing for Shankly's team, but the story went that if he did leave Elland Road, Leeds would be seeking a transfer fee in the region of £30,000 to compensate them for their loss. So they must have thought something about him.

In the event, Liverpool didn't land Jack Charlton - much to his great disappointment. Some years later, he was to figure in the Leeds United side which went to Wembley and came up against Shankly's outfit in the final of the FA Cup. It was a final which Leeds were to lose, after extra time.

Liverpool that afternoon fielded a team which included centre-half Ron Yeats, whom Shankly *had* signed for around £30,000. He had been a slaughterman in an Aberdeen abbatoir, was big in stature and, when Shankly held a Press conference, was introduced as "a colossus."

Yeats played a key role in Liverpool's glory years of the 1960's, as they won the FA Cup for the first time in their history, claimed the League championship after having gained promotion, and went to the semi-finals of the European Champions Cup. Had Shankly stepped in to land Jack Charlton from Leeds United, there could well have been a totally different story not only for Ron Yeats (later to return to Anfield as chief scout), but for the lad from Ashington who believed his career at Elland Road was going nowhere fast.

As it was, Charlton remained at Leeds, somewhat dispirited and disillusioned, and not at all enamoured of the prospect of having to join in a desperate battle as the Elland Road club came face to face with the dreaded prospect of relegation to the Third Division. Little did he realise then that the pendulum would be swinging completely the other way, in his favour.

Leeds were to profit from a partnership off the field which turned the ailing club into one of the most formidable forces in British football - its team feared abroad, as well as respected (and, at times, rather reviled) on the domestic front. The partnership involved two men: self-made millionaire Harry Reynolds, and debutant manager Don Revie, a man whom Jack Charlton finally learned not only to like and to trust, but a man who also earned a big vote of thanks for having set the centre-half on the road to stardom.

As for Harry Reynolds, he could speak his mind, just like Jack Charlton and Don Revie. I got to know him a bit during his time as chairman of Leeds United and on one occasion, in fact, he and I were dinner companions, along with Sir Matt Busby and Alan Hardaker, who was then the secretary of the Football League. The occasion was a meeting of UEFA in Portugal, and we dined in the plush Palacio Hotel in Estoril. The conversation was enlightening, to say the least.

Harry Reynolds, like Jack Charlton, was a smoker; he smoked cigarettes, and he used to carry them around in a battered old tin. There were no false airs and graces about him - he could call a spade a bloody shovel with the best of them, and when he said his piece, people listened. This blunt-talking Yorkshireman once went out on to the pitch at Elland Road and told the fans where they got off.

At the time, the supporters were voicing some criticisms of the way results were going, and the Leeds chairman decided it was up to him to give them a few answers. He didn't mince his words, either, as he referred to the sniping which had been going on. He told the critics that the board and the manager were well aware of what was required, and that the manager had the confidence of the directors. When the manager reckoned he had found the right players, the board would put up the cash to sign them.

Reynolds, indeed, told the fans that being the chairman of a soccer club was far from being a sinecure, and if anybody felt that he could improve upon the job that Harry Reynolds was doing as chairman of Leeds United, then he was welcome to try his hand at it. So far as I can recall, there were no takers.

The Leeds fans considered that they had a case, of course. They had seen other clubs snap up various players for fees ranging from around £70,000 to £100,000, and they had also seen their team being subjected to a couple of hammerings. West Ham, for one, had stuck no fewer than seven goals past the Leeds 'keeper, while Liverpool had cashed in on that disaster and pumped five goals into the United net.

Harry Reynolds had come into the Elland Road club at the worst possible time, because not only were Leeds struggling to get results on the field, they were not exactly flush with money, either. Sufficient to say that Reynolds, having taken on the job of chairman, demonstrated that he WAS prepared to put his money where his mouth was, and before he had finished, he was having the last laugh.

As a businessman, he knew what he was doing, and he quickly got to grips with the job of running a football club. Raich Carter, Bill Lambton and Jack Taylor had come and gone, and the next incumbent of the hot seat faced problems all the way round, even allowing for the fact that Harry Reynolds was ready, willing and able to come up with money for new faces in the dressing-room.

The choice fell upon a man who had played for Leeds United, among several other clubs. It was a choice which raised a few eyebrows in football, because the newcomer had no experience at all in the art of management. When the name of Leeds United's new team boss was revealed, players who had known him as one of their team-mates instantly wondered how he, and they, would react to what had become a changed situation, virtually overnight.

The new manager had arrived at the Elland Road club at a time when his distinguished career as a player was clearly coming to an end. He had then cost more money than any other British footballer when you added up all the transfer deals in which he had figured (he had played for five different clubs), and don't laugh when you see what the overall amount was. Added up, the transfer fees totalled £83,000!

As a player, he had obviously garnered more than a few headlines during his career; as a manager, he was very much on trial. But inside a matter of a few years, he was to transform Leeds United from being a club bound for obscurity into one which scaled the heights. His name was Don Revie.

I first got to know Don Revie when he was a player. At that time, he was wearing the colours of Sunderland, and I drove up from Manchester to the North-East to talk to him. He struck me as being a regular sort of bloke: straight, intelligent, and wary of giving away too much to nosey-parker journalists. I got to know him well in later years, and I always found him all right. We never had a problem in our dealings, although there was one occasion when I felt it was pertinent to point out that I, and some of my colleagues, hadn't been enamoured of the way we had been treated at a Leeds United function.

In fact, we hadn't been snubbed, but although we had been invited to the celebratory "do", we had not exactly been overwhelmed by the warmth of our welcome. A similar thing happened when I attended an Everton championship dinner at a plush hotel in Liverpool. The gentlemen of the Press were all seated at one table, and we hadn't been asked to bring wives or girl friends, as the players and officials had been invited to do.

On that occasion Alma Cogan was the cabaret artiste, and at one stage she held up her hand and informed the assembled audience that if people didn't stop talking while she was trying her best to entertain them, then she would stop singing. That shut them up.

When I told Don Revie of the way the gentlemen of the Press felt, he immediately took my point, and gave me to understand that it wouldn't happen again at any future occasion for celebration, and as the years went by, Leeds United had plenty of cause to celebrate.

In later years, when Don Revie had become the England team manager, he and I met at a function where he was the main guest speaker, and he indicated to me that he expected to be speaking for around half an hour. I had gone along with David Lloyd, the

Lancashire county cricketer and England Test batsman, who was also billed to speak, and when I mentioned what Revie had said to me, the organisers were a little dismayed, and had obviously expected the England team boss to be on his feet for more than 30 minutes.

I don't know if anything was said to him, but to his credit Don stood up, and talked for considerably longer than half an hour, and had his audience in stitches as he delivered story after story about his experiences in football. To be honest, I became a little bit worried about how the audience would receive David Lloyd, after this top-of-the-bill performance by the England manager. In point of fact, David had them rolling in the aisles, too, when the theme switched from football to cricket.

When Jeff Powell broke the story in the Daily Mail that Don Revie had defected from Lancaster Gate to take up a soccer job in the Middle East, the world of football was agog. Peter Swales, who as chairman of the England international committee worked closely with Revie during his time as the international team boss, told me that Revie had found it hard going. Swales offered the opinion that "the job of managing England is the most difficult job in football.'

Revie might not have been cut out to be what, in effect, was a part-time manager; certainly he was cut out to be a successful team boss when involved in the day-to-day running of a club. On the other hand, it's been suggested that Jack Charlton's forté is being an international team boss, rather than having to go through the daily grind of striving for success at club level.

So far as I know, he never got the chance to manage Leeds United, never mind England, but it's interesting to speculate what might have happened had he become "the boss" at Elland Road. Would Leeds have tasted success sooner than they did, rather than having to wait many long years until Howard Wilkinson came along? Or would Big Jack have jacked it in after a relatively short interval, as he did when he turned his back upon Newcastle United, the club he had followed as a lad? We'll never know, of course.

What is certain is that Don Revie, who revived the fortunes of Leeds United, also rescued the career of Jackie Charlton, at a time when the big fellow was probably at the lowest point in all his footballing career.

A Turning Point

Don Revie knew just what it was like to be regarded as a rebel. Indeed, during the later days of his career in football, he knew also what it was like to become the target for the tabloids as a manager who had turned his back on his country. Maybe, just maybe, when he became the team boss at Leeds United, that reputation he once had as a rebel (during his time as a player with Manchester City) goes some way towards explaining why he took the time and trouble to get Jack Charlton's career back on the rails, even if it meant telling the centre-half some home truths in the process.

Revie was steeped in football; he had played for Leicester City, Hull City, Manchester City and Sunderland before he joined Leeds United, still as a player. He had also married the boss's niece, which meant that Elsie Revie knew her soccer, too; her uncle, Johnny Duncan, managed Leicester City.

It was Don Revie's arrival at Elland Road which marked a turning point in the fortunes of Leeds United, as well as in the life of Jack Charlton. By the time Leeds signed him, Revie could claim to hold the record of having cost more in transfer fees than any other British player. The £83,000 total looks ludicrous now, compared with the £5M Blackburn Rovers splashed out on Chris Sutton.

Revie, as I have said, had also gained a reputation of having been a bit of a rebel. There came a time when he and his club couldn't see eye to eye with each other, and the dispute made headline news, with Revie reported to be training on his own.

It was in 1962 that Don Revie was given the chance to try his hand at managing a football club, and it meant that he had to make an immediate transition from being a player, and a team-mate, to being "the boss." Not surprisingly, the players who had been his team-mates at Leeds were all curious to see just what kind of a job he would make of it, and they also wanted to know how he would react to them.

One minute, he had been "Don", and the next he was the

guv'nor who was telling them what to do, after chairman Harry Reynolds had handed him the job of trying to work a near-miracle in not only putting the club back on an even keel, but by bringing trophies to a club starved of success.

In the process, Don Revie had to convince the men who had been his team-mates that he would give them all a fair crack of the whip, and in Jack Charlton's case there was the memory of what Revie had said to him on one occasion when they were team-mates. Remember... "The best thing that could happen to you would be for the club to leave you out, you're spoiling it for others, with that chip on your shoulder. You'd never do for me."

When Don Revie took charge of team affairs, Leeds United were, to put it mildly, sinking; sinking, in fact, towards the Third Division. So he needed all the help he could get from his senior players, and that included Jack. Big Jack confessed to me later that it did indeed take him the best part of a year to feel easy in his mind about having Revie as his boss, and to realise that the manager was ready, willing and able to give him a fair crack of the whip. Even though there were still a few home truths to be handed out!

Revie surrounded himself with backroom men he felt he could trust: coaches Syd Owen and Les Cocker, and chief scout Maurice Lindley. Owen had been a key player in defence for Luton Town when they lost against Nottingham Forest in the 1959 FA Cup final, and he and Big Jack had more than one brush before Charlton "saw the light." Jack related to me how he and the coach failed to hit it off, and how they almost came to blows on one occasion.

Remarkably, however, in a matter of weeks the "chip" that Revie had talked about was disappearing from Jack's shoulders, and an entirely new relationship began to be built up between player, manager and coaching staff.

Syd Owen had what Jack termed a "disconcerting" effect upon him at the start. The first time they encountered each other, Owen took him by the arm and asked him what was the problem between himself and Leeds United. Jack admitted to me that he was churlish as he answered, but despite being more or less told to "shove off", the coach wouldn't give up on him.

He spoke quietly, but his words were straight and to the point. He asked Jack Charlton to put a transfer out of his mind and to give the backroom men a chance. "If you decide you still don't like us, after a while, you can ask to be put on the list again."

One of Big Jack's grumbles was about the way the players had trained in the past, and his mood hadn't been improved by the way Syd Owen used to shout at the lads during practice matches. Owen's shouted criticisms tended to raise Jack Charlton's blood pressure, and he lost his temper on one occasion, offering to "take his coat off" to the coach, and warning the manager that if Syd Owen didn't get off his back, "I'll not be responsible for my actions!"

It's difficult to imagine any of the players who went to the World Cup in the Summer of 1994 threatening to "take their coats off" to Jack Charlton the manager; that's a prospect which tends to make you smile at the likely outcome. But back at Leeds, Don Revie listened and heard Jack out, though Syd Owen didn't change his style.

All in all, it was a salutary experience for Jack Charlton and, as he told me, one which made him realise something. "Looking back, I needed discipline," he said. And if he got it, he also came to realise that here were backroom men who were ready to work until they dropped in the effort to improve the ability of the players under their command. And if the training had become harder, it had also become much more interesting; no longer did Jack Charlton feel reluctant to head for Elland Road in a morning.

Jack discovered that if he went about it the right way, he could have a very good future as a professional footballer, and he realised that he had reached a turning point. Revie, Owen, Cocker and Lindley between them played a key part in steering him towards what was to become a long-running international career.

While Jack Charlton was beginning to change his tune with regard to Leeds United, Don Revie was becoming somewhat desperate to halt the slide towards the Third Division, and so, in March 1962, he took a calculated gamble. He made a bid of £25,000 for an inside-forward who had been regarded as one of the finest players in the land, but who, according to some people, was coming to the end of a glittering career.

The player in question was wee Bobby Collins, who had been signed from Glasgow Celtic by Everton. Bobby stood around five feet five inches tall, and he wore size four-and-a-half boots; he was a "pocket general" whose chunky frame concealed a giant-sized heart. He had skill in abundance, a razor-sharp brain, and the courage to go with it. He feared no opponent.

However, when Don Revie made his bid, he knew that Bobby Collins had reached the age of 30, and in those days that was a real landmark in a player's life. In fact, there used to be a joke that a footballer had a "playing" age, as well as his real age; in short, he always reckoned to take two or three years off his real age, when anybody asked him how old he was.

Bobby Collins had been the "king" at Goodison Park, and it came as somewhat of a surprise to learn that Everton were prepared to dispense with his services. Their manager, Harry Catterick, however, felt that he was doing good business, because after several seasons of great service from the wee man, Everton would be recouping every penny of their original outlay. It was Leeds who were taking the gamble.

As it happened, I knew Bobby Collins well, well enough, indeed, for him to give me a call and tell me the shock news about Leeds having made an offer. Bobby wanted to talk about the matter, and he was looking for some advice. I lived near Manchester, which was the half-way house between Merseyside and Leeds, and so I told Bobby: "Look, if you're going over to see Don Revie tomorrow, come and stay the night at my place." That was on a Wednesday, and Bobby duly drove over from his home in Aintree.

He had been a bit taken aback when he was informed of the bid from Leeds, and even more surprised when he had been told: "We're ready to let you go." But he was a realist, too, so he was ready to consider the move.

When Bobby arrived at my home, we discussed all the implications of joining Leeds, and we talked for hours. My final advice to him was this: "Go through to Leeds tomorrow, talk to Don Revie, but whatever else you do, DON'T sign for Leeds. Once people know that you're up for sale, who knows which other clubs might come in?"

Obviously, one of the most important things from Bobby's point of view was the fact that Leeds looked perilously close to sliding into the Third Division, and, of course, he had been playing top-level football with Everton. No way did he want to sink into Division 3, yet, on the other hand, this was a challenge for him, to give Leeds United the kind of lift they so desperately needed.

My final words to Bobby on that Thursday morning were: "Remember what I've told you. Listen to them, ask for time to think it over, if they want you badly enough, they'll wait a few more days." I knew, as Bobby knew, that Leeds would want him signed before five o'clock that afternoon, otherwise they wouldn't be able to put him in their team the following Saturday.

Bobby indicated that he would take my advice and follow it to the hilt. "Give me a ring when you get back home today, and let me know how you've gone on," I told him. And he did give me a ring, to tell me: "I'm speaking from Leeds, and I've just signed for them." My answer to that bit of news was short, and to the point: "You bloody fool!"

Bobby, however, had the last laugh, because as things turned out he could not have made a better move, neither could Leeds United have made a better signing. Here was a player who made an instant impact, a player whom Jack Charlton came to admire greatly; indeed, Big Jack certainly learned something from the wee man.

Leeds agreed that Bobby could travel through a couple of days a week for training, and do some training on his own back on Merseyside. A lot of folk thought this was a ridiculous arrangement, and they said so, but they didn't know their Bobby Collins. As Jack Charlton and Bobby's other new team-mates soon found out, they had got themselves a fitness fanatic. The way he went about his job inspired players years younger than him to work all the harder.

When he wasn't training or playing football, Bobby would be back home, often spending a couple of hours each afternoon resting in his bed. At all times he made sure he retained that sharp edge of physical fitness so necessary for a professional footballer; he reckoned he could carry on playing at top level until he was near 40. Even when he was into his 50's, to my knowledge, Bobby continued to keep fit by training regularly.

While he was with Leeds, he actually made a come back after having a thigh broken during a match in Turin (his team-mates were incensed about this injury which had been inflicted upon him), and while in his mid-thirties, he went to Wembley with Leeds to play in the 1965 FA Cup final against Liverpool. But the main thing this Scottish international footballer did was to help Leeds secure their status in the Second Division, then gain promotion and honours at home and in Europe.

Had Leeds United gone down at the start of the 1960s, Don Revie would probably never have been given the chance to manage England or maybe, even, to manage another club, and Jack Charlton and his team-mates would have sunk with the club - in some instances, probably, without further trace. As it was, inspired by Bobby Collins, Leeds United prospered, and so did Jack Charlton.

Don Revie then assembled some rare talent, much of it home-produced. He was a stickler for attention to detail, too. Peter Lorimer, who, like Bobby Collins and Eddie Gray, became a Scotland international, set a record as the youngest player ever to appear in Leeds United's first team, in September, 1962. At the time he was 15 years of age. Other clubs had been on his trail, but Don pipped them all by driving up to Lorimer's home to win the race; he even got stopped for speeding! By the time Lorimer got to bed, it was three o'clock in the morning, and the Leeds manager was on his way back to Yorkshire.

Billy Bremner, as well as Peter Lorimer and Jack Charlton, was another player over whom Revie took a tremendous amount of trouble, and not just because Bremner acquired something of a reputation as a fiery little character. Like Jack Charlton, Bremner wanted away from Leeds during his early days; he pined to be back home in Stirling.

It was Bill Lambton who could claim the credit for having taken Bremner to the Elland Road club, and this in spite of the fact that he had become a target for Arsenal, Chelsea and Glasgow Celtic. Indeed, Bremner, having spent a couple of weeks enjoying the sights and sounds of London, as well as the hospitality dispensed by Arsenal and Chelsea, had made up his mind to give it a go at Parkhead when, almost out of the blue, Leeds United's manager and the chairman, Harry Reynolds, appeared on the scene.

From all accounts, they had sat up and taken notice of Billy Bremner when he had been playing for Scotland boys against England, whose side included Terry Venables, the current international coach. But Lambton and his chairman hadn't been at the match; they had watched the proceedings on television!

So Billy went down to Elland Road to see what he thought about Leeds, and they persuaded him to throw in his lot with them, only to find, not long afterwards, that he was homesick. But just as he was on the point of sticking out for a move back north of the border, he won promotion to the reserves, and then, when he got itchy feet once again, word filtered through that he was in with a chance of making his first-team debut, against Chelsea.

He was just a couple of months past his 17th birthday when he went out at Stamford Bridge, and his partner on the right wing that day was none other than Don Revie, who was shortly to become his boss. Revie took Bremner under his wing: they were room-mates in the London hotel where the team stayed, and he made sure that it was bed-time at nine o'clock on the Friday evening. A few days later, Bremner and Revie were team-mates again, this time in a friendly against Hull City, and Revie was booked.

By the time Don had taken over as manager, Bremner was still "doing a Jackie Charlton", unsettled, and hankering after a transfer. And when he asked to go and heard that Hibernian were ready to fork out £25,000 for his services, he thought that was that, until Leeds insisted on a fee of £30,000. So Bremner had to soldier on. Even so, he didn't give up on his quest to shake the dust of Elland Road off his feet. Time and again, he tried to convince Don Revie that a transfer would be the best solution for himself and the club.

Behind it all was the fact that Billy Bremner's girl friend, Vicky, lived and worked in Stirling, so the Leeds United manager decided to take action. He drove up to Scotland to see Vicky and talk things over with her, then she began to talk to Billy about set-tling down in Yorkshire. The upshot was that he did just that and, eventually, he married Vicky and they set up home in Leeds.

As for Jack Charlton, the player who, by his own admission, had been "a one-man awkward squad", he began to knuckle down as well. And Don Revie, who, as a player, had told Jack: "If I were a manager, I wouldn't have you in my team!" (or words to that effect) began to tell the lanky centre-half: "You should be playing for England, if only you would have the sense to do yourself and the club justice." Fortunately for Jack Charlton, they were words of wisdom which he heeded.

And as time went by, so Leeds United's players knitted togeth-er as a team. Having landed Bobby Collins, they also signed a wee Irishman by the name of Johnny Giles, and eventually he took over the mantle of Collins as the "general' of the side. More than a few people thought that when Don Revie paid Manchester United £40,000 of Leeds United's hard-earned cash for Giles, he was gam-bling too much; but in the end Revie and Leeds wound up with another winner.

While Bobby Charlton was a team-mate of Nobby Stiles at

Old Trafford, Jack Charlton became a team-mate of Nobby's brother-in-law, Johnny Giles, at Elland Road, where the impish Irishman, whom many had dubbed as a skilled player, but one who was maybe "too nice" during his time with the Manchester club, demonstrated that, deep down, he also possessed a streak of tempered steel in his make-up.

As for Jack Charlton, he still hadn't quite come to regard himself as an automatic first-team choice, and there was a very good reason for this: suddenly, there was talk that Leeds United intended to bring the great John Charles back from Italy. It would be a move calculated to gratify the fans, of course, and it would certainly bring about an improvement on the playing side.

Big Jack's worry was that "The Gentle Giant" could play up front or at centre-half, and while Charlton by that time had (or thought he had) established himself in the No.5 jersey, now there seemed a prospect of his having to battle all over again to stake his claims to that shirt.

One day, the players went out golfing and, as if he had read Jack Charlton's mind, Don Revie took the big fellow to one side to tell him: "I'm not going to move John back to centre-half, you're there, and you're staying there." It was a tremendous vote of confidence for Jack, and after that, the only way to go was up, into the international arena.

"If you played the game right and did the job you're supposed to do, you would be playing for England." Those words rang through Jack Charlton's mind and fired his ambitions. Deep down, he had always considered himself to be a pretty decent player, but his confidence had been eroded at times. Now he had the right incentive to put everything into the job of making his mark on the international stage, and he proceeded to do just that.

Under Don Revie, Leeds began to go places. They avoided the drop into the Third Division, were able to concentrate upon getting out of the Second and into the First Division. Along the way, Don Revie and his backroom henchmen groomed soccer talent which was to take the club to the pinnacle; indeed, there came a time when Leeds, like Matt Busby's Manchester United, could field a team of internationals, and still leave one or two out.

In goal, there was the Welsh international, Gary Sprake, and if he once let the ball slip through his hands and over the goal line while the Anfield Kop chorused "Careless Hands", he certainly proved that overall he was an extremely competent 'keeper. Behind him came another top-class goalie, David Harvey, who eventually took over from Sprake.

The back-four line became automatic: Paul Reaney, Paul Madeley, Jack Charlton, Terry Cooper, while in midfield Leeds had the likes of Billy Bremner, Norman Hunter and Johnny Giles (following on from Bobby Collins). Up front there was the subtle wing play of Eddie Gray, the bullet-like shooting power of Peter Lorimer, the goal-poaching of Allan "Sniffer" Clarke, the equal menace of Mick Jones, and more besides.

Revie, the man who paid such attention to detail, did a remarkable job in a relatively short space of time as he welded his players not only into a formidable force on the field, but into a footballing family off it. When he became the manager of the England team, Revie was sometimes derided for his efforts to instil the same kind of atmosphere at the players' get-togethers, but it certainly worked well at club level.

Revie himself had been honoured with the Footballer of the Year award while he was playing for Manchester City in season 1954-55; his senior coach, Syd Owen, had claimed a similar honour while he was with Luton Town in season 1958-59, and now, at Leeds United, the honours were coming to the players under Don Revie's command.

In season 1964-65, Bobby Collins followed Bobby Moore, who was shortly to lead England to World Cup glory, as the Footballer of the Year; 12 months later it was the turn of Manchester United's Bobby Charlton to carry off the prestigious award; and 12 months after that, Jack Charlton, Bobby's elder brother and the man who had been such an awkward customer at times during his Elland Road career, was walking up to receive the coveted award at the annual luncheon in London. As for Don Revie, he was named Manager of the Year in successive seasons, 1968-69 and 1969-70.

By that time, he had seen his Leeds United lads climb out of the Second Division as champions, go to the final of the FA Cup on a couple of occasions, carry off the League Cup, and win the European Inter-Cities Fairs Cup. And to cap it all, they had clinched the League championship at the end of season 1968-69, with an all-time record haul of 67 points and only two defeats behind them during the campaign. It was a record of which Revie could well be proud and, as he told me: "One day some team will win the title with more points, but I doubt if we'll see any side go through a season again with only a couple of defeats."

It was indeed a tremendous pity that Don Revie's own managerial career should end amid such controversy, as he left these shores for the Middle East, and that he later suffered from the motor neurone disease which cost him his life. Leeds United tried to keep the managerial job "in the family", much as Liverpool did when Bill Shankly bowed out, but it proved a task too much for the men who followed.

It was said that when Revie left Elland Road, he recommended that Johnny Giles should be installed as his successor. That didn't happen, the controversial Brian Clough was appointed, and his reign lasted just 44 days before it ended in sensational fashion, with talk of a massive golden handshake and suggestions that the men who had played under Revie didn't give the new arrival their backing.

Duncan McKenzie, the first player Clough signed for Leeds (along with John O'Hare and John McGovern, who had played for him elsewhere), told me that he never felt the Leeds lads showed any resentment against Clough, although he believed the old stagers at Elland Road had been disappointed that Giles didn't get the job. Duncan told me: "Despite Revie's departure, there was a certain amount of Revie still within the heart of the club; you couldn't simply dismiss his influence, after all the time he had spent with those players there."

True enough. And after Clough had gone, others tried their hand at the toughest job in English club football: Jimmy Armfield, who took Leeds to a European Cup final; Jimmy Adamson, Jock Stein, then the bid to bring back the glory days by giving the job to someone who had been "in the family." Billy Bremner, Eddie Gray and Allan Clarke were all given the chance to make it work. Bobby Collins told me later that he felt two of these three would have made it work had they been given more time.

Collins himself, like Johnny Giles, missed out on managing Leeds United, as did Jack Charlton. One wonders if he would have been the man for the job, but, as things turned out, Leeds had to wait until the start of the 1990's before Howard Wilkinson could deliver the League championship to the Elland Road club once again.

By that time, Big Jack had established himself as a manager on the international stage with the Republic of Ireland, and there is little doubt that had Don Revie been able to witness the progress his one-time awkward customer had made, he would have smiled with genuine pleasure, and it would have done his heart good to see what Jack Charlton had made of himself. Footballer of the Year, Manager of the Year - in that respect he had followed right in Revie's footsteps.

Lost Causes - And Success

When David Harvey became Leeds United's first-team goal-keeper, he was not too big to give praise where praise was due. He admitted, for a start, that in his early days at Elland Road he was inclined to take things as they came. It was Syd Owen, the coach with whom Jack Charlton tangled, who quickly changed Harvey's attitude, as well. "He made me realise I couldn't hope to succeed in professional football if I adopted such an attitude; he did such a good job of work on me that now I'm always up and doing, trying to perfect my game."

Harvey also praised team-mate Jack Charlton for the way the big fellow tried to shield him and keep opposing forwards at a distance, so that the 'keeper could gather the ball unchallenged. "It's that sort of team spirit at Leeds," said Harvey.

It was the sort of team spirit instilled into his players by Don Revie, and it took Leeds United into the First Division and into the final of the FA Cup against Liverpool, in 1965. Jack Charlton won't forget that final, even today, nor will he forget three matches, two of them Cup finals, against Chelsea.

First, the 1965 final, which was won by Liverpool after extra time. It wasn't rated as one of the classic finals, although from a Liverpool point of view there were no complaints: Bill Shankly became the first team boss to have managed a Liverpool FA Cup-winning side, and he did the trick again in 1974, when Liverpool defeated Jack Charlton's boyhood favourites, Newcastle United.

In season 1964-65, Leeds United and Liverpool were big guns together. Liverpool had come out of the Second Division and, like Leeds, they were staking their claims to honours at home and in Europe. In 1965 Leeds were aiming for the classic double of First Division title and FA Cup, and they went mighty close to achieving their ambitions.

As it turned out, they had to settle for second-best in both competitions, but they certainly gave it their best shot. Not that Leeds were everybody's favourites at the time. Indeed, so far as some people were concerned, they were the whipping boys, because critics branded them with the tag of "dirty Leeds."

They were accused of having kicked their way out of the Second Division, and there is no question about it, the Leeds manager and his players resented such accusations. Yes, Leeds United played it hard, after all football was a physically competitive game and there was no room in it for fainthearts. But it hurt the players that their critics couldn't see the genuine talent there was in the side.

However, Leeds United's battlers - there was a sign in the dressing-room which said "Keep on fighting" - knew that in the final analysis there was one answer, and that was to win trophies along the way. They proceeded to do exactly that, although at first it appeared as if they were destined to be the nearly-men of football.

In the chase for the championship, Leeds had five games to go when they came unstuck against Manchester United, who went to Elland Road and scored the only goal of the game. That was the beginning of the end, so far as visions of the championship were concerned. The following Monday Leeds went to Hillsborough and lost there against old Yorkshire rivals Sheffield Wednesday.

Next came the return match against Wednesday, and this time out the result went Leeds United's way. They scored another victory when they met Sheffield United at Bramall Lane, but on the Monday in the week they were due to meet Liverpool at Wembley, they had to take on Birmingham City at St. Andrews. That was United's fifth match in the space of 10 days, and it turned out to be too much for them.

At one stage of the match Birmingham were leading by three goals, then Leeds were awarded a penalty, and Johnny Giles got them back into the game with his spot-kick. It was Jack Charlton who struck next, so then there was only one goal in it. Urged on by Don Revie, the Leeds players got stuck in and Paul Reaney went upfield to score and make it 3-3, but, try as they might to snatch a fourth goal, which would have ensured the title, Leeds had to settle for the draw. So they were pipped for the championship by Manchester United, who managed to beat Arsenal by the only goal at Old Trafford and, thereby, became champions by virtue of their superior goal average.

Apart from being accused of strongarm tactics, as it were,

Leeds didn't endear themselves to the fans of other clubs by their willingness to play the game right to the limit. What it boiled down to was that they played within the rules, but went to the very edge, and at one stage a bit of a fuss was made about the way Leeds United and Jack Charlton in particular acted at corner kicks.

Today, everyone recognises the value of set-pieces, and teams practise ploys at free-kicks and corners until, sometimes, they're almost too clever for their own good. The Leeds creed, under Don Revie, was simple enough: fight for the ball in a game of physical contact, and don't shirk it. In other words, when you go for the ball, go for it with the firm intention of winning it.

This, then, was the idea when Big Jack went upfield and into the opposition's goalmouth for a Leeds United corner kick. Since a player cannot be offside at a corner kick, Jack went up and stood on the opposition's goal line, ready to do the necessary when the ball came across, the necessary being to put the ball into the net with his head.

With players such as Giles and Gray in their ranks, Leeds knew that they were able to rely upon the men taking the corner kicks to plant the ball precisely. So the plan was for Jack Charlton to wait, and as the ball was dropping for him, to give it the final nod with his napper and hey presto! It was a goal. It was a ploy which worked extremely well, and Jack scored his fair share of goals from this kind of situation, much to the annoyance of the opposing goal-keeper.

The 'keeper often claimed that by standing on the goal line, the Leeds centre-half was impeding him and preventing him from getting even a sight of the ball as it came over. The 'keeper also claimed that as Jack went up, it meant that he was obstructing him from being able to catch the ball, and, on occasion, the 'keeper also claimed that Jack Charlton backed into him.

Big Jack's reply to all this was that he was playing within the laws of the game; that he wasn't committing any kind of foul; that he wasn't obstructing anyone, simply doing his job, and let the referee be the judge of what was and what was not illegal. He pointed to the fact that referees almost invariably allowed the goal to stand, in which case, Jack Charlton couldn't have done anything wrong.

It's worth pointing out that Leeds were not the only team using such a tactic at dead-ball situations: Liverpool used big Ron Yeats,

Manchester United sent Bill Foulkes upfield for corner kicks, and so on and so forth. Maybe, Jack argued, he'd done better than most when it came to sticking the ball in the net, and, in any event, it was up to the opposition to work out ways and means of countering the Leeds United tactics.

What no-one seemed ready to point out, also, was that Jack Charlton was prepared to take the knocks in his efforts to score a goal, and many times he returned to his home in worse shape than when he left it.

In view of the way that FIFA clamped down during the 1994 World Cup, it does make one wonder just how many bookings and sendings off there would have been under those conditions when Leeds United were making their presence felt during the 1960s and the 1970s. Yet when Jack Charlton was managing the Republic of Ireland team and directing their strategies during the Summer of '94, there didn't appear to be any complaints about the way his men played the game, so he got something right, even if he fell foul of FIFA in what could be termed a touchline war of words.

But to get back to 1965 and the FA Cup final against Liverpool, Leeds went straight from Birmingham to London, and for once the tactics of Don Revie in this respect were questioned by some of his players, who felt that five days away from home before a Wembley date was too long.

Leeds United certainly didn't come up to expectations against Liverpool, who managed to score the first goal, thanks to Roger Hunt. Once that had happened, Leeds pushed Billy Bremner upfield, and he managed to restore the balance as he struck an equaliser. He was ready to get back in defence then, with his sights on a replay, but it was decided that he should stay up, in the hope that he would snatch a winner.

That distinction fell to a fellow-Scot, Ian St. John, during extra time. Unfortunately, St. John happened to be one of Bill Shankly's players, so the Leeds dream of an FA Cup triumph to compensate for that championship letdown, was shattered. And the players reflected ruefully that what their chairman, Harry Reynolds, so often said was indeed true: "You get nowt for coming second."

There were three more FA Cup occasions which, from Jack Charlton's point of view, turned out to be non-events, and each of them concerned a club from London - Chelsea. Leeds United had hoped to make a swift return to Wembley, but the following season

there was more disappointment to come for Jack and his team-
mates.

For the second time in succession, they finished as runners-up
in the championship chase, while in the FA Cup, after having stuck
half a dozen goals past the Bury goalkeeper in the third-round tie at
Elland Road, Leeds met their masters at Stamford Bridge. That
was a Cup-tie which, like the 1965 final, has lingered in Jack
Charlton's mind.

Chelsea got their noses in front, despite everything that Leeds
could do, and after that it was a case of trying to hold out as the men
from Elland Road threw everything at their opponents. Leeds continued to attack, with Jack Charlton upfield as the minutes ticked
away towards full time, then, in the dying seconds of the match, he
found himself clean through the Chelsea defence and with only
'keeper Peter Bonetti to beat. Jack let fly, and the shot went straight
to the Chelsea 'keeper. The chance to salvage something out of the
Cup-tie had been lost.

And so to the 1970 final of the FA Cup, when Leeds United
and Chelsea met once again, this time at Wembley.

By the time the final was played, Everton had pipped Leeds for
the League title, Billy Bremner had been named as Fooballer of the
year - and Leeds had had to overcome Manchester United in two
semi-final replays to reach their Wembley goal. Jack Charlton was
up against brother Bobby; Bremner put the skids under the Old
Trafford outfit with a goal which came, overall, after 219 minutes
of play, and, to put the icing on the cake, at long last the fans around
the country were starting to applaud Leeds for their fluent style of
football.

Having lost an Elland Road duel with Glasgow Celtic in the
semi-finals of the European Cup, as well as missing out on the title,
Leeds United went to face Chelsea at Wembley determined to put
on a show. It turned out to be what hardened critics labelled as one
of the finest finals in the history of the FA Cup . But it didn't bring
Jack Charlton and his team-mates victory.

The pitch was not the usual, immaculate Wembley turf: it had
been sanded, and players were almost ankle-deep in mud and sand
at times, yet the players of both teams contrived to turn on some
exciting football. And with Giles spraying passes around, Leeds
got on top, so that the traffic became one-way towards the Chelsea
goal.

Twenty minutes into the match, Leeds were one up, and Jack Charlton played a vital part in the goal, which came as the result of a corner. As the ball came across from the right, there was the Leeds centre-half doing his usual stuff and rising above the Chelsea defence to nod the ball towards goal.

There may not have been a tremendous amount of power behind his goalbound header, but it was sufficient to send the ball looping down between a couple of Chelsea defenders who were standing on the line. As each man swung a foot at the ball, it seemed that one of them must be sure to connect, but to Big Jack's delight, the ball simply bounced between the pair of them, then rolled over the goal line.

Shortly before half-time, however, Chelsea scored an equaliser as Peter Houseman collected the ball outside the 18-yard box and drilled a low diagonal shot which went through a ruck of players and under Gary Sprake's body.

The second half largely followed the pattern of the first, with Chelsea doing the defending and Leeds finding that 'keeper Peter Bonetti was barring the way time and again. Leeds could thank Sprake for a couple of fine saves, and Jack Charlton for a goal-line clearance which certainly had a touch of genuine class about it. Jack was facing his own goal, but he looked as cool as a cucumber as he took the ball, controlled it, then swung round and walloped it away.

With seven minutes to the final whistle, Leeds thought they'd cracked it, as Allan Clarke dived to send in a header. The ball cannoned back off a post, however, but Mick Jones was on the spot to deliver a low shot which went straight into the far corner of the net. This, it seemed, must be the killer goal, the one that won the FA Cup.

Yet Chelsea showed that they were not quite finished, as they drove forward and made a final fling. They won a free-kick, which was taken quickly by John Hollins, and as the ball sped goalwards, Ian Hutchinson flung himself at it and got a touch with his head, to leave Sprake stranded and the Chelsea players leaping about in delight.

It was the World Cup final of 1966 all over again for Jack Charlton - denied a victory in the dying minutes and condemned to extra time. And as it turned out, for the first time in 58 years, a replay was necessary in the final of the FA Cup.

Players had gone down with cramp under the testing conditions, and now they had to drag their weary legs through another tortuous half-hour of labour. Not surprisingly, neither side could force an advantage, and so, with the half-hour completed, it was still stalemate. The players of both sides made their way up the steps to the royal box, where Princess Margaret was waiting to greet them, but there were no medals, and there was no presentation of the FA Cup.

Finally, the Leeds and Chelsea players summoned up the energy to complete a lap of honour, then they parted company for the time being, knowing full well that they must go through it all again the following mid-week, this time not at Wembley, but in the cauldron of Manchester United's Old Trafford.

On the night of Wednesday, April 29, 1970, in company with thousands of other people, I made the trek to Manchester United's ground to see if Leeds United, having been pipped at the post the previous Saturday at Wembley, could finally see off Chelsea in the battle for the FA Cup. What we all saw was a duel which Chelsea won in dramatic fashion, after a gruelling slog which had lasted 240 minutes altogether and left Leeds with nothing, save total disillusion.

It seemed, indeed, as if Leeds were fated to finish second-best, because they had got their noses ahead twice in the Wembley encounter, only to see their opponents bounce back and snatch equalisers; and at Old Trafford, which was packed for the occasion, the fans saw Leeds dominate the game yet again. But that was a night which ended in absolute misery for the men from Elland Road.

Some people reckoned it was an omen when Leeds had to make a change, with 'keeper Gary Sprake dropping out after having failed to recover from an injury, and David Harvey replacing him. Harvey was no novice, though, and he was a good 'keeper; he had gone on as the substitute for Leeds when they played Glasgow Celtic in the semi-final of the European Cup at Parkhead, and manager Don Revie gave him a firm vote of confidence on the eve of the FA Cup-final replay.

So the Leeds team looked just as strong as ever it did: Harvey in goal, Paul Madeley and Terry Cooper at full-back, Jack Charlton flanked by Billy Bremner (who became another Leeds record holder with 54 caps for Scotland) and Norman ("Bites yer legs")

Hunter. As for players who could stick the ball in the net, Leeds could point to Peter Lorimer (famed for his deadly shooting), Allan Clarke (the man they called "Sniffer", because he was always on the scent of a goal), hard-working (and often under-rated) Mick Jones, Johnny Giles (the general) and Eddie Gray (silken skills allied to scoring ability).

That team was virtually an all-international eleven, and, like Johnny Giles and Allan Clarke, Mick Jones had proved he had been worth his £100,000 fee, although it has to be said that when Don Revie signed Jones from Sheffield United, this wasn't the player he had really been seeking.

He had gone to Bramall Lane originally with the idea of per-suading United to part with another striker, Alan Birchenall, but when he realised that it would be almost impossible to talk the Bramall Lane club into letting Birchenall go, he settled for switch-ing to Mick Jones. There came a day when Jones was named by Sir Alf Ramsey in a 40-strong England squad, while Birchenall, who by then had been sold to Chelsea for £100,000, was finding himself on the outside, looking in at Stamford Bridge.

When Leeds and Chelsea met in the 1970 FA Cup final, there was a touch of irony in the situation: while Jones helped his side outplay the team from Stamford Bridge, Birchenall was on the sidelines, he couldn't even find a spot as a Chelsea substitute. Which brings us back to the Old Trafford replay, and another intriguing aspect of the situation.

Glance again through the team that Leeds United put out that Wednesday night, and it doesn't take long to realise that here was a side consisting almost totally of home-produced talent. True, Jones had cost £100,000, Clarke had been an even costlier import by Don Revie (he had splashed out a record fee of £165,000 to land him from Leicester City), and Giles was a comparatively modest £40,000 buy from Old Trafford.

While Eddie Gray and Peter Lorimer, along with Billy Bremner, wore the dark-blue jersey of Scotland, England could call on no fewer than half a dozen of the Leeds players lining up against Chelsea: jack-of-all-trades Paul Madeley, (who turned down the chance to go to the World Cup finals in Mexico in 1970), left-back Terry Cooper (who could also do a stint on the left wing), centre-half Jack Charlton (on occasion, a valuable asset also as a marks-man), Norman Hunter (defender or midfielder with a bite), and

Clarke and Jones as a striking combination. It was said that strikers hunt in pairs, and these two certainly forged a formidable force up front.

If Leeds had Harvey replacing Sprake in goal, Chelsea also had to make some changes, because their rising midfield star, Alan Hudson, was another who failed a fitness test. This meant that Chelsea had to do some switching around, especially when it came to containing winger Eddie Gray, who had given right-back David Webb, now Brentford's manager, a torrid time in the first duel at Wembley.

The second time around, at Old Trafford, it was Chelsea skipper Ron Harris (nicknamed "Chopper") who took over the right-back spot, in order to keep a close watch on Gray, while Webb wore the No.6 jersey. The enigmatic, Scotland-international star Charlie Cooke played at inside-right, and another player with charisma, Peter Osgood, lined up at centre-forward, with Ian Hutchinson, famed for his long throw-in, at inside-left and Tommy Baldwin and Peter Houseman on the wings.

In goal, Chelsea had the reliable Peter Bonetti, and with Ron Harris they had the dependable Eddie McCreadie, plus John Hollins and John Dempsey, which meant that the substitute's job went to Marvin Hinton, with Mick Bates the player figuring in a similar role for Leeds.

From the outset of the replay, Leeds went on the attack, as they had done at Wembley, and while "Chopper" Harris stuck closely to Eddie Gray, Mick Jones and Peter Lorimer began to emerge as the men who might turn the battle Leeds United's way. Lorimer was using his pace to get down the right flank, turn the ball past McCreadie, then put across centres which posed danger for the Chelsea defence, while Jones, despite the close attentions of Dempsey, caused problems on the ground and in the air.

The longer the first half went on, the more assured Leeds United seemed, while Chelsea's hopes of taking the FA Cup back to London began to appear doomed to failure. David Harvey found himself in the position of the fans who packed the ground: he was virtually a spectator, as play was concentrated in the Chelsea half of the field.

With the game about 30 minutes old, the ball was curled into the Chelsea goalmouth for the umpteenth time, and as Bonetti rose to the occasion, so did Jones. These days, goalkeepers are protected almost to the ultimate degree, but twenty-odd years ago challenges such as this one were commonplace. However, Bonetti was injured in the collision, and he required attention to his knee, so that he was still left hobbling when play was resumed.

Not surprisingly, in another battle for possession, it was Jones who won the ball and, with nine minutes to go to the interval, he put Leeds United ahead.

It was Clarke who started the attacking move as he shrugged off the attentions of three defenders then slotted a pass through to his striking partner, who then took on two opponents, forced a gap between them and rammed in a scoring shot. Bonetti said later that he did manage to get his hands to the ball and that, had he not been feeling the effects of the earlier injury, he might well have pulled off a save.

But as things stood, Leeds had taken the lead, just as they had done at Wembley, and few people in the Old Trafford audience doubted that they would maintain their superiority during the second half of the match. Once again, when play had resumed, it was Leeds who dominated, and it seemed only a matter of whether or not they could score more goals. But fate hadn't finished with Jack Charlton and his team-mates yet.

During the last 20 minutes of the game, Chelsea began to assert themselves, while Leeds seemed to have lost the incentive to keep up the pressure. Twelve minutes from full time, Chelsea managed to pull off another reprieve, as Cooke got the ball and realised that he had a bit of space, for once. He turned on his best style, feinting and weaving his way past Leeds defenders, then he delivered a pass aimed for Peter Osgood.

The Chelsea striker was unmarked and on the alert, and he wasted no time: he simply took off and, as his body sped through the air, his head made contact with the ball, which flashed past Harvey and into the net. All of a sudden, Leeds had been deflated and Chelsea's players were jubilant. They could sense that yet again they had pulled off a miraculous escape, and this time they might even get a winner.

Jack Charlton and his team-mates might be down, but they were not prepared to give up. Once they had got to grips with the changed situation, they followed the precept of the notice which hung in the Elland Road dressing room: "Keep on fighting." Indeed, they attacked the Chelsea goal in a frantic flurry during the last five minutes of normal time, camping out in the penalty area and almost on the goal line itself. But when the whistle blew, it was still stalemate, at 1-1.

During extra time there were some bone-crunching tackles from players on both sides, as they overcame tiredness and fought to prise another goal out of the opposition. The end of the first period was looming; there were, perhaps, 60 seconds left on the clock, when Chelsea got their chance to turn the tide. They were awarded a free-kick, and the long throw-in reached David Webb, despite the despairing efforts of Jack Charlton to get his head to the ball as it went across the face of the Leeds goalmouth.

Webb, indeed, was virtually "doing a Jackie Charlton", for there he was, standing practically on the Leeds goal line, and when he nodded the ball past 'keeper Harvey, he had given his team the lead for the first time in 224 minutes of football. It was a lead Chelsea were not to surrender; that goal proved to be the one which killed off Leeds.

After having been ahead twice at Wembley and once at Old Trafford, the Leeds players were fighting to draw level, and time was running out. Chelsea's players, and the crowd, now sensed that the final had reached its turning point, and that was how it turned out. Leeds strove in vain to breach the Chelsea goal during the second spell of extra time, but when the whistle went at last, match-winner Webb and his team-mates collected the FA Cup.

So Jack Charlton sat in the dressing-room and pondered on the might-have-beens; pondered, too, on how Chelsea in particular appeared to have been a bogey-team so far as he was concerned. He could look back upon a season in which Leeds had been going for what people had called "the impossible dream": a treble of League championship, European Cup and FA Cup. Everton had taken the title from Leeds, Glasgow Celtic had triumphed in the semi-finals of the European competition, and now Chelsea had demolished the hopes of the Leeds players that they would find consolation in the FA Cup.

But, of course, it hadn't been a case of lost causes all the way along the line. Big Jack could look back, also, upon a championship triumph achieved in genuine style at the home of their greatest rivals at club level - Liverpool. For this was where he and his team-mates had clinched the championship on a previous day, to the ungrudging acclaim of the Anfield Kop.

That, truly, had been an occasion for Jack to savour, especially since Leeds were in hot competition with Bill Shankly's men, plus Everton and Arsenal, for the trophy which proves that the winners are, without question, the best side in the country. It was a title race which was dominated by Leeds United, Liverpool, Everton and Arsenal, but by the time Easter was coming up, the men from Goodison Park and Highbury looked to have too much to do, although leaders Leeds had seen their rivals from Anfield starting to breathe down their necks.

While Leeds were drawing against Wolves at Molineux, Liverpool were winning their match in London against Queen's Park Rangers; then they were held to a draw by Arsenal at Anfield, with Leeds getting a similar result against Sheffield Wednesday at Hillsborough 24 hours later. And on Easter Saturday, it was Liverpool versus Wolves at Anfield, Leeds against the current champions, Manchester City, at Maine Road.

Roger Hunt scored the goal that put paid to Wolves; Johnny Giles did the the same thing to City. With half a dozen matches to go, Leeds had 58 points, and Liverpool, with seven games to play, remained five points adrift, yet Leeds had to visit both Liverpool and Everton towards the end of April. If results went against Leeds and in favour of Liverpool, Shankly's team could finish up one point in front, or it could even depend on goal average.

As well as having to play twice on Merseyside, Leeds had to travel to London and try conclusions with Arsenal at Highbury; that was a game in which, Liverpool hoped, Leeds would slip and stumble. But at Highbury, it was the Gunners who went down by the odd goal in three, and then came the match at Goodison Park, where 59,000 people flocked to see what would happen.

Should Everton win, they would be giving their Merseyside rivals a leg up, especially if Liverpool, playing the same night at Highfield Road, managed to beat a Coventry City side struggling desperately for safety points. At the end of both matches, though, not one goal had been scored, so it left Leeds on 64 points with 40 matches played and Liverpool still five points behind, but with a game in hand. Meanwhile, Arsenal and Everton were fighting it out as to which of them claimed third place.

Leeds, of course, were the favourites: even if Liverpool should win all their remaining matches, they could total no more than 65 points, while Leeds, with a home game against Nottingham Forest, as well as the match against Liverpool at Anfield, required just one point by then. Leeds were going flat out, also, to take their tally of points to 67 and thus set a record for the championship.

For Leeds and for Liverpool, the Anfield confrontation was the crunch, and Don Revie's team knew full well that Shankly would exhort his men to go for victory. The match drew 53,750 people to Anfield, and when they had closed the gates, there were still a couple of thousand fans locked out.

As the match progressed, with every player fully committed, there were times when Liverpool looked like scoring: Alun Evans, the first £100,000 teenager in football, passed up a couple of chances, while the "daddy" of the team, Ian Callaghan, fired one drive wide, then forced Gary Sprake to pull off the save of the game. The final whistle, however, signalled the end of hostilities and the crowning of Leeds United as the new champions.

Despite the fact that there had been no goals, the game was a thriller, and at the end, the Leeds players found themselves being saluted by the Kop. While Liverpool were in with a shout, the Kop fans were in full voice, urging their own favourites on, but once the die had been cast, they hailed the Leeds players as they did a lap of honour around Anfield. Bill Shankly went into the Leeds dressing-room to tell the players: "You're worthy champions - a great side."

As for Jack Charlton, he now looked back on a remarkable Leeds record which he had helped in no small way to build. Since Leeds had climbed out of the Second Division, they had played 209 matches and won 119 of them. Defeats? They had suffered only 39! In half a dozen seasons they had won the Second Division championship, the Football League Cup, the Inter-Cities Fairs Cup and the championship of the First Division.

Big Jack hadn't quite finished his career at Elland Road, but when the time did come for him to bow out, he could be well satisfied.

He had played a major part in the rise of Leeds United to eminence. Since they emerged from the Second Division as champions, their First Division record had been equally impressive: second, second, fourth, fourth and then first. At long last, they could claim that they did indeed have an honours list, even if they had missed out on a season which had promised so much: a glittering treble of League title, FA Cup and European Cup.

Jack Charlton and his team-mates had given the Leeds fans

something to shout about, and not before time, as the club's honours list demonstrated so clearly. It read like this:

1924 - Second Division champions.

1964 - Second Division champions.

1965 - First Division runners-up and FA Cup finalists.

1966 - First Division runners-up and semi-finalists in the Inter-Cities Fairs Cup tournament.

1967 - Finalists in the Inter-Cities Fairs Cup and semi-finalists in the FA Cup.

1968 - Winners of the Football League Cup and the Inter-Cities Fairs Cup; semi-finalists in the FA Cup.

1969 - Champions of the First Division (only two defeats, and a record haul of 67 points).

1970 - Finalists in the FA Cup and runners-up in the First Division, semi-finalists in the European Cup.

In a personal sense, there was every reason for pride, as manager and players collected individual awards: 1965 - Bobby Collins, Footballer of the Year; 1967 - Jack Charlton, Footballer of the Year; 1970 - Billy Bremner, Footballer of the Year. And in 1969 and 1970, Don Revie, Manager of the Year.

Leeds United could also boast at that time that they could field a team of players who had won representative honours, like this: Gary Sprake (Wales), Paul Reaney, Jack Charlton, Norman Hunter, Terry Cooper (all England); Terry Yorath (Wales), Billy Bremner (Scotland), Johnny Giles (Republic of Ireland), Eddie Gray (Scotland); Mick Jones and Allan Clarke (England).

When Leeds went so close to the treble in season 1969-70, they had to play virtually every game as if it were a Cup-tie, so keen were rivals to knock them off their perch - don't forget, they were the champions who had set new standards in domestic football. They had to supply players for international duty and still keep going at club level, and they also had to meet what in effect was an end-of-season deadline, because immediately afterwards, the World Cup campaign in Mexico was looming.

Even so, Leeds ran Everton close for a title repeat, and Everton themselves fell one point short of the Leeds record as they amassed a total of 66 points. In the process, they suffered five defeats, as did Leeds United, although in their case three of those matches were lost in the dying stages of the season, when the pressures were greatest and time, as much as the opposition, was the enemy. Yet Leeds still contrived to score more goals than Everton, the new champions, or than anyone else in the four divisions of the Football League, and while they had to be satisfied with a total of 57 points, they also knew that this had been sufficient to claim the championship in the past.

By 1970, of course, Jack Charlton (and Don Revie) were heading for the close of their careers as manager and centre-half at Leeds United, and they were to go their separate ways: Revie into a less-than-satisfactory stint as the international team boss after Sir Alf Ramsey, Big Jack into club management, which brought him considerable success and, at times, a sense of something less than fulfillment.

"Wor Bobby"

By the time he was seven years of age, Jack Charlton's younger brother, Bobby Charlton, was already showing signs of developing into a very good footballer. Indeed, Cissie Charlton became convinced in her own mind, even then, that his name would become famous in the professional game. No doubt this was the same sort of instinct that prompted another shrewd judge to predict that Bobby Charlton would one day play for England.

That particular judge was a fellow by the name of Joe Armstrong, and he happened to be the chief scout of Manchester United. One session of watching Bobby was sufficient to impress Joe, although he did tell me later that after the youngster had arrived at Manchester United to be put through his paces, not everyone agreed with this assessment. In fact, Joe confided to me that there was a school of thought at Old Trafford which believed Bobby wouldn't go all the way to the top, and that it might even be doing him a favour to allow him to return to his native North-East.

However, Joe's instincts, like those of Cissie Charlton, proved to be correct. Bobby, who was playing with and against lads twice his age even before he had reached his teens, was born with the body-swerve and turn of speed which enabled him to glide past his opponents, and if Cissie used to tell him off for risking life and limb against lads who were approaching the age of 20, it made no difference. As she said to me: "Bobby would just smile and say that I shouldn't worry about him getting hurt, 'I'll be all right', he used to say." And he was.

He lived for football, and when he wasn't playing, which was not often, he would accompany big brother Jack to watch the real professionals in action, which meant Roker Park or St. James' Park.

However, while Jack was a devotee of Newcastle United - a club he was later to manage, and to shun - the players whom Bobby idolised wore the strip of Sunderland, and deep down there was the hope that when the time was right, he would receive an invitation to try his luck at Roker Park. When the brothers went into town, before going to the game, they dined in what used to be called the British Restaurant, which was a relic of the war-time days. The cost of the lunch they enjoyed was what used to be known as two and a tanner, or half a crown. In todays's currency, that's all of 22$\frac{1}{2}$p.

At holiday times, Bobby would travel south to Chersterfield to stay with Cissie's brother, George, one of his footballing uncles, and he spent as much of his time as possible training with the professionals. Spending money in those days was 5p. a week - this went up to 22$\frac{1}{2}$p. when Bobby had reached the age of 14. It was not long before he was earning considerably more money than that as a footballer himself, however.

Joe Armstrong was the man who first popped the question about Bobby's future as a footballer, and he talked to Cissie Charlton about it. I can just imagine Joe, a genial little fellow with a persuasive tongue and an engaging smile, telling Bobby's mother all the ins and outs of what going to Manchester United would mean.

The first time I ever talked to Joe, a retired civil servant, was when he telephoned me at my own home to ask if I would allow my son, then still at school, to go down to Old Trafford's training ground during the holidays. He had obviously watched him play football, not just for the school team but for the county side, and he figured that he was worth having a look at.

I can remember my son arriving home and buzzing with excitement as he imparted the news that "I've been playing two-touch with Denis Law and Bobby Charlton!" Ultimately, however, and despite Joe Armstrong's keenly-expressed interest in him, he didn't embark upon a professional career with Manchester United. But Bobby Charlton did.

Not that United was the only club chasing his signature: along came Sunderland, Liverpool, Manchester City and Wolves, but, by that time, it was all too late. Bobby had opted to go to Old Trafford and, since he was by then attending Bedlington Grammar School after having passed his scholarship, there was the little matter of further education to be sorted out.

Manchester United agreed that he could continue his studies at Stretford Grammar School, which was little more than a stone's throw from Old Trafford, but that notion soon went out of the window. Only a few months after Bobby had arrived in Manchester, he wrapped up his scholastic career and concentrated upon the talent he had in both feet. It was a talent that blossomed over the years, although both Bobby and Cissie Charlton were to undergo some traumatic moments in their lives before they were finished.

I refer to what has long been known simply as the Munich disaster, which occurred on Thursday, February 6, 1958. Like Bobby Charlton, I had a personal interest in this tragedy, because, like him, I could so easily have been caught up in it. I was working in Manchester as deputy sports editor of the The People newspaper, and it was planned that I should travel with Manchester United when they went to Belgrade to play Red Star in a European Cup-tie. Incredibly, I had all but packed my bag ready to leave when my boss reported sick, so this meant that I would have to miss the trip in order to man the office.

There but for the grace of God...

Among the victims who never returned were fellow journalists whom I knew well: Henry Rose, my old boss at the Daily Express; Tom Jackson, with whom I had worked at the Manchester Evening News; Eric Thompson, of the Daily Mail; George Follows, of the Daily Herald; Alf Clarke, of the Manchester Evening Chronicle; Archie Ledbrooke, of the Daily Mirror; Donny Davies ("Old International"), of the The Guardian; and Frank Swift, the one-time England goalkeeper who had gone to Belgrade for the News of the World.

One journalist who had earlier been a colleague of mine, Frank Taylor, then on the old News Chronicle, lived to tell the tale, although his injuries left him with a limp. Indeed, a report of his death was actually published because of a mix-up over a passport which had been found among the wreckage on the airstrip at Munich.

The players who perished were captain Roger Byrne, Liam Whelan, Duncan Edwards, Eddie Colman, Tommy Taylor, David Pegg, Mark Jones and Geoff Bent (who had helped to teach my wife to drive), while secretary Walter Crickmer, trainer Tom Curry and coach Bert Whalley also died, as did two crew members and two passengers - one a travel agent, the other a racehorse owner who was also a keen United fan.

Then there were the survivors: Johnny Berry, Jackie Blanchflower, Harry Gregg, Bill Foulkes, Kenny Morgans, Albert Scanlon, Dennis Viollet, Ray Wood - and Bobby Charlton. Matt

Busby himself lay at death's door for a while, but he made an amazing recovery. As for Bobby Charlton, he ended up in the Rechts der Isaar hospital in Munich, like "the boss."

Harry Gregg and Bill Foulkes had the task of identifying survivors, and while the former identified Ray Wood and Foulkes did the same with Johnny Berry, the doctors were working overtime, operating and trying to save lives. At one stage, Bobby Charlton passed out and was given an injection. Eventually he, with the others who had lived to tell the tale, came home again to play football, although, like Matt Busby, he went through a stage where he wanted to turn his back on the game.

When I went to see her in Ashington, it was inevitable that at some stage in the conversation about her sons Cissie Charlton should be reminded of that dark day at Munich. And I learned from her that on the morning of the crash she awoke with a feeling of premonition that trouble was brewing. "I felt in my bones that something was wrong." she said. "All through the morning, I had a premonition of disaster."

She left her home in Beatrice Street and went to chat to a neighbour about United and their scheduled return from Belgrade. "They're flying home today; I wish they were home now," she said. Down at Elland Road, Jack Charlton had gone training, so he had little time to dwell upon other things, though briefly, as he told me later, he thought about Bobby and United coming home.

Up in Ashington, where Bobby's father had returned from the night shift at the pit, Cissie Charlton left her husband to sleep soundly on, even as she worried and fretted that something bad was about to happen. When she looked out at the back of the house and saw the man from the corner post-office walking up the yard, she knew her worst fears had been realised: something bad HAD happened.

Her first words to him were: "It's the plane, isn't it?" And then she learned about the crash, or, at least, the little that was known at that moment in time. Unknown to Cissie Charlton, Jack was preparing to leave Elland Road after training when he heard about the crash. Then he caught the first train up to Newcastle.

Across the Continent, Harry Gregg and Bill Foulkes had been able to phone the British consulate and ask them to let the people back home know about the survivors, and up in Ashington, after what seemed an eternity, the local police constable turned up at the

Charlton household smiling and waving a scrap of paper. It was a message from the Foreign Office, and it said that Bobby was safe. He had managed to contact a German journalist who in turn had got in touch with the Foreign Office, and Bobby's message: "I'm all right", had been relayed to the police in Ashington by phone.

Jack Charlton hadn't arrived at his parents' home at that stage, and he learned about his brother's survival when he arrived at Newcastle railway station and bought an evening paper. Bobby's name was there, in the stop-press column.

Cissie Charlton, having heard the good news along with the bad, phoned Matt Busby's right-hand man, Jimmy Murphy, who promptly invited her to go down to Old Trafford, where there was plenty of work for willing hands. "We'll find you something to do," Jimmy told her, adding: "It will help to take your mind off things." So down she went, to do all kinds of jobs as the need arose, while she awaited the return of Bobby from Munich.

Once he was on his way back, Cissie and her eldest son went by car to meet him, and the reunion came at Liverpool Street station in London, during the early hours of a Sunday morning. They drove back to Leeds, then Bobby and his mother caught the train to Newcastle. During the journey he talked about the horror of Munich, then told her: "Now I want to forget all about it."

I gather that Bobby Charlton has seldom referred to the Munich disaster since, although when, after his return home, he was asked about his future plans, he made it clear that they didn't include football any more. That decision, which seemed irrevocable, was changed after a kickabout with a schoolboy pal at a local park. Bobby regained his enthusiasm for playing, and he broke the glad news to Jimmy Murphy in a phone call to Old Trafford. Jimmy told him: "You can come back straight away, son."

Those were emotional days, as I can vouch for from personal knowledge. For instance, I travelled with Manchester United to Milan for their next European Cup-tie, shortly after Munich. We went overland - by train from London to Dover, by boat to Calais, by train to Paris, where we boarded the Simplon-Orient express, and, after having slept on the train, we arrived in Milan early on the Monday morning. My travelling companion - we shared a compartment with two couchettes - was young Ronnie Cope, a reserve centre-half who, like several others, had been pitched into first-team action after the team had been decimated at Munich.

United lost in Milan, but I was there the night they were swept to victory on a tide of emotion in an FA Cup-tie at Old Trafford; Sheffield Wednesday (the opposition) never really had a chance. True, they had their supporters, but the rest of the country, like the United faithful, willed the Manchester men, Busby's Red Devils, on to victory.

Bolstered by new signings (Ernie Taylor from Blackpool, Stan Crowther from Aston Villa), and a leavening of experience (Foulkes) plus the virtually-untried new boys, United progressed in the FA Cup until they reached the final itself. They went to Bispham, near Blackpool, for training and stayed at what was then the Norbreck Hydro, where I saw Matt Busby appear as he joined Jimmy Murphy and his players. Matt was hobbling and needed two sticks as he made his way down the drive of the hotel.

He resisted the advice of those who told him not to travel to Wembley for the final against Bolton Wanderers (which United lost), and this was the team which United put out that Saturday afternoon: Gregg, Foulkes, Ian Greaves, Freddie Goodwin, Cope, Crowther, Alex Dawson, Taylor, Charlton, Viollet and Colin Webster.

When United had played Sheffield Wednesday things were so much up in the air that the club couldn't even give the names of the players who would be in United's line-up, so they didn't appear in the programme for the match, which was played on a mid-week night. When United went to Wembley to fail gallantly in their attempt to win the Cup, Cissie Charlton was there to see her son in action.

She told me how Matt Busby had invited her to join the official party for the after-match banquet, and how, when he saw her there, he discarded his walking sticks as he hobbled across and spoke to her. There were tears in Matt's eyes as he stroked Cissie Charlton's hair and embraced her, saying softly: "Thank God, thank God that Bobby was spared."

It was Matt's wife, Jean, who urged him to carry on at a time when, in the aftermath of Munich, he felt that he could no longer continue to manage Manchester United or even retain a connection with football. "Those boys who have gone would want you to carry on," she told him. And Cissie Charlton felt, too, that the survival of her son was a factor in Busby's final decision to rebuild the team. At the time of Munich, Bobby Charlton was little more than an up-

and-coming teenager, although people had started to take notice of him as a player.

The story of Bobby's progress to world-class footballer has become a part of soccer history: Footballer of the Year at the end of season 1965-66, European Footballer of the Year, World Cup winner with England and winner of a European Cup medal with Manchester United.

Jack Charlton described his brother as looking like "a little boy lost" when he returned from the Rechts der Isaar hospital in Munich, and I always felt that the shadow of the tragedy appeared to be hanging over him. So often did he present a solemn visage to the world, even though he could summon up a smile when the occasion merited it.

In 1966 Bobby was a member of the England team which triumphed over Portugal in a classic World Cup semi-final; in 1968 he was a member of the Manchester United side which became the first English club to carry off the European Champions Cup by defeating Portuguese opposition once more, in the shape of Benfica, the Eagles of Lisbon. In 1966 and 1968, that great player, Eusebio, was on the losing end, while Bobby and his brother Jack celebrated success.

For Bobby and Eusebio, there were tears for souvenirs: Bobby had shed them after the World Cup win, and after United had defeated Real Madrid in their European Cup semi-final, while Eusebio had also shed tears after Portugal's World Cup exit.

The World Cup had been won at Wembley, and it was at Wembley that Bobby Charlton and Manchester United scored their European Cup success against Benfica - with Bobby having the extra pleasure of scoring in a match which first of all see-sawed, then finished up with United overwhelming the opposition.

In the first half, a vicious drive from Eusebio had cannoned off the United crossbar. A goal then, and Benfica would have had their tails up. Eight minutes after the restart, Bobby Charlton was giving United the lead in a manner which few would have forecast, because he scored with a header. And heading, as he freely admitted, was never one of his strong points.

He also experienced a feeling of déjà vu as Benfica equalised, just as West Germany had done in the World Cup final, so that the European Cup final also went into extra time. And but for 'keeper Alex Stepney, who during the second half had made a superb save to deny Eusebio, United would surely have been down and out.

It was George Best who made the scoreline 2-1, Brian Kidd (celebrating his birthday) who made it 3-1, and Bobby Charlton who put the icing on the cake as he flicked a cross from Kidd past 'keeper Henriques to get his name on the scoresheet twice and ensure that United won by a final margin of 4-1.

On such a night of glory the players found the energy to do a lap of honour around Wembley, but the occasion had left Bobby Charlton drained. He went straight from the post-match reception for both teams (it was held at the stadium) and returned to United's hotel, to climb into his bed. Then he missed the rousing reception when United returned to Manchester, because by then he was on his way to play more football, this time for England, who were competing in the European Nations Cup.

He was not to know, then, that the day would dawn, after he had hung up his playing boots for good, when he would follow Matt Busby on to the board of directors at Manchester United, and follow in Busby's footsteps also as a knight, honoured for his services to the game of football. By that time, in the Summer of 1994, Bobby's name had become revered throughout the world, and his record with club and country had more than stood the test of time.

Altogether during his career at Old Trafford, he had played 751 games for Manchester United in the years between 1954 and 1973, and totalled 245 goals, while at international level he had struck 49 goals in 106 appearances for England. He had overtaken the record of the great Billy Wright when, in a World Cup match against West Germany in Leon, Mexico, he had clocked up his 106th game for his country. That was in June, 1970, and the record stood until Bobby Moore won his 107th cap when he played against Italy in Turin, in June, 1973.

The Charlton tally of 49 international goals put him one ahead of Gary Lineker, five ahead of Jimmy Greaves, and 19 ahead of both Tom Finney and Nat Lofthouse, although Nat's 30 goals came in but 32 England appearances, while Finney played 76 times and Greaves 58 times.

It was recorded about Bobby that "he remains a modest man; the courtesy drilled into him in a Geordie working-class environment has remained with him." It was further recorded how, in the Munich disaster, "he was flung 40 yards from the wreckage of a

crashed airliner" and how he survived to become "a legendary footballer and one of the finest roving ambassadors this country has
ever known."

When Bobby Charlton was awarded his knighthood, he was
already the holder of the OBE and the CBE, and he had been a
director of the Old Trafford club for a decade. How, indeed, does
time fly! The knighthood was "the ultimate prize for a man who
has winner's medals for the World Cup, the European Cup, the FA
Cup, three First Division championships plus 106 England caps, as
well as the OBE and the CBE."

Charlton's response to the honour of a knighthood: "You can
win the World Cup yourself, but you can't do this. This is your
country honouring you. I feel very humble." Bobby had had to
keep the news of his latest honour secret for several weeks, and
that, he admitted, was "very difficult."

Norma, his wife of 33 years, said that Bobby had been thrilled
because he had been knighted for his services to soccer - "he still
loves every aspect of the game." Brother Jack said Bobby was
"one of the best players in the world for a long time. I had a call
from London about his knighthood this morning (he was speaking
from his World Cup base in Orlando), and I'm not at all surprised
about it. I've expected for some years our kid would be knighted."

Jack added: "He deserves it. They knighted Stanley
Matthews, Alf Ramsey and Matt Busby, and Bobby has been a
great ambassador for his country ever since he finished playing in
the early seventies. We get on pretty well, although, like all brothers, we have our differences, at times. But our kid remains a thoroughly decent, upstanding fellow who is a credit to himself."

Whenever I talked to him, Jack Charlton never gave the slightest indication that he resented or was jealous of his younger brother's success, although in their playing days, at club level, they were
competitive. I recall Jack telling me how, on one occasion, Bobby
got the better of him and he yelled with delight: "I've nutmegged
you!"

One of the remarkable things about the relationship between
the two footballing Charltons is the fact that each, in his own way,
has been so successful. Bobby Charlton has been a household
name the world over for many years and, as Jack said, he has been
an excellent ambassador for the game and for his country. Yet by

the Summer of 1994, when Bobby was being knighted and Big Jack was taking the Republic of Ireland team into the last sixteen of the World Cup, it was arguable which of the brothers had become the more famous.

Michael Hyland, president of the Football Association of Ireland, surely echoed the thoughts of many other people when he said he believed there should be a unique double, with Jack joining his brother as a knight of the realm. Hyland said: "Jack was a highly popular man in England before his achievements with Ireland, they should take that into account. If the powers-that-be were compassionate, they would make him a knight, too. In fact, they should make him a Lord for his services to football."

I could just see Jack Charlton (having been appointed an honorary Irishman by the Irish Parliament, and having succeeded in taking his Irish team to the World Cup after failing to click for the England job) smiling broadly, if also somewhat wryly, at that one.

Continental Capers

There was a fellow called J.B. Priestley who could write a bit, and he offered the opinion that the game called football was, in fact, a matter of "conflict and art." Liverpool manager Bill Shankly was known to say that football wasn't just a matter of life and death, it was more important than that.

Then there was Edson Arantes do Nascimento - Pélé, to you - who called football "the beautiful game", while the late, great Danny Blanchflower, who captained Tottenham Hotspur to the classic League-FA Cup double at the start of the 1960's and who led Northern Ireland to a spell of brief glory during the 1958 World Cup in Sweden (where Pélé, at the age of 17, first made his mark on the world stage) termed soccer "a game of imagination and improvisation."

I could well imagine anyone who asked Jack Charlton for his description of football being greeted with a somewhat lop-sided smile, as the pugnacious-jawed Geordie replied: "....ing hard work!" That's not to say he hasn't enjoyed his time in the game; knowing him, if he hadn't enjoyed it, he would have quit long, long ago. But he has experienced just about everything that football can offer, its lows, as well as its highs.

Jack has always recognised that it's an extremely physical game, and no doubt he can still recall the occasion when Leeds United were playing Manchester City, and he went upfield to find himself surrounded by no fewer than eight opponents in the City penalty area.

His team-mates were surprised. Indeed, Billy Bremner expressed his amazement that Big Jack, despite being so outnumbered, somehow stretched that long neck of his and got his head to the ball, to nod it past the City 'keeper. There were folk who referred to Jack Charlton as "the giraffe" because of that neck, and there was an occasion, also, when it appeared that he had something in common with the elephant: a long memory.

That was when he came out with talk about having "a little

black book", and everyone took this to mean that Jack had noted down the names of people in the game with whom he had a score to settle. Some folk expressed indignation at Jack, if this should be the case, but the big fellow merely smiled in enigmatic fashion, and I don't think anyone ever discovered whether or not he had indeed compiled a "black list" of those who had offended against him. Maybe it was just a Charlton wind-up, to frighten off anyone who thought of putting the boot in.

Jack never shirked a challenge on the field, and the were times when, after he had been well and truly clobbered, he would return to his home almost black and blue with bruises. It's interesting to speculate what the men of FIFA, who ordered a clampdown by referees during the 1994 World Cup, would have felt about the way things sometimes went during Jack Charlton's playing career.

For instance, the time Bobby Collins had his thigh broken during a match against Italian opposition, or the time when Jack Charlton was given his marching orders, when Leeds United came up against opponents from Spain. It was Billy Bremner who admitted that he played with murder in his heart when he saw Collins chopped down so cynically in a game against Torino in Italy.

Leeds were competing in the Inter-Cities Fairs Cup, and according to Bremner - no softy himself - the foul was just about the worst he had ever seen on a football field. Bremner was a fiery customer (he and Kevin Keegan were sent off by referee Bob Mathewson when Leeds and Liverpool met at Wembley in a Charity Shield match), and the Scottish international actually shed tears of rage when he saw his fellow-countryman lying on the ground with his thigh bone broken.

Collins, then turned 30 years of age, was rushed to hospital, and it was feared that the injury - according to his outraged teammates, the foul had been committed 10 yards distant from the ball - would spell the end of a fine career. Remarkably, the wee man not only recovered to be able to walk properly again, but he actually came back to play first-team football for Leeds United. Like Billy Bremner and Jack Charlton, he was a hard man.

Big Jack became the victim of a refereeing decision during another match in the Inter-Cities Fairs Cup. This time the game was being played at Elland Road, and the opposition from Spain was provided in the shape of Valencia. True to form, Charlton went upfield and into the Valencia goalmouth every time Leeds were awarded a corner kick.

Not surprisingly, in such a competitive match, he had taken his fair share of buffeting as he tangled with the Valencia defenders, but he hadn't shown any reaction, until an incident which really made him see red. Valencia had managed to get their noses in front during the match, which was played only a few months before England staged the 1966 World Cup tournament, so Leeds United were hell-bent on getting an equaliser.

As their own supporters roared encouragement to them, they attacked in waves, and the Valencia defenders resorted to some desperate measures in a bid to prevent Leeds from grabbing an equaliser. At last, however, the home side managed it, and then they went looking for a winner. It was at this stage that Jack Charlton made another sortie upfield, and as he challenged a Valencia player in the Spaniards' goalmouth, he received a kick, followed by a punch, for his pains.

It was said at the time that Jack went berserk, certainly he was seen to be chasing opponents around the penalty area. The sequel was that three players, including Charlton, were shown the red card, and the referee called both teams off the pitch so that the players would have some time for their tempers to cool. Even then, there was a war of words which continued long after the whistle had been blown to signal the end of what had been a frenetic and ill-tempered Cup-tie.

Afterwards, Jack admitted that he had lost control of himself, and that his sole thought was to extract vengeance for the assault upon his person. Billy Bremner recalled, in fact, that at one stage during the fracas Jack was surrounded by half a dozen Spanish players, and that when he thrust his way into the fray to help his team-mate out, he found himself being collared by one of the policemen who had gone on the pitch to bring about some form of order.

As the copper hauled Bremner away towards the touchline, the Leeds player heard him caution: "Now, Billy lad, take it easy, don't go getting mixed up in any trouble!" And trouble there was, all right, with Dutch referee Leo Horn, a veteran of 130 international matches outside Holland, adding fuel to the fire with his remarks.

Horn walked off with his linesmen, signalling that the players of both sides should do the same, and the teams were off the field for 11 minutes, in which time they were supposed to cool their tempers. When they returned, Jack Charlton and Valencia left-back Garcia Bidagany were missing. They had both been given their marching orders, and before the end of the match the Spaniards' inside-forward, Sanchez-Lage, had been dismissed for having kicked Jim Storrie.

The game ended with the score 1-1 and referee Horn declaring that Bidagany had indeed been the originator of the trouble when he kicked Jack Charlton. But he also said that "Charlton's reaction went beyond mere provocation." On Jack's behalf, Don Revie said: "He was provoked; he was kicked all through the game." And he declared that he had been right when he had said Valencia were a tough team - "they're one of the worst we have ever played."

By the time referee Horn had returned to Holland, he was being quoted as saying that Leeds were on a bonus of £1,500 to win, and that "money was the cause of the trouble. You could see it in the nervousness and the excitement of the players. There was something in the air, something unpleasant. There was too much at stake. It was unbelievable." So ran the quotes attributed to him.

He was also said to have been reminded of cup finals he had handled in South America, where players were on a 3,000-dollar bonus. "Since European football began, we have seen this sort of thing spreading.

These games have become too important for the players. When Leeds lost a goal this nervousness spread among them. Valencia had nine men in front of their goal. They, too, were gripped by this terrible feeling." Horn claimed that he understood professional footballers, but said they had changed. "Money has made them too eager. After 16 years of international refereeing, I believe money causes all the trouble, all the nervousness and desperate play. It is no use clubs expecting referees to impose discipline, the referee is there to control a match. Players must be taught to control themselves."

One wonders what Leo Horn would have thought about the FIFA edicts in the 1994 World Cup, when referees were expected to produce the yellow card almost at the drop of a hat.

On a more personal note, when it came to Jack Charlton, Horn was quoted as saying: "I have always regarded Charlton as a fine man. He was the cleanest player on the field, until he lost all control. I saw a Spanish defender kick him, and if Charlton had given a reprisal kick I could have understood and let it pass, because it happens so often. As captain of Leeds, and an international, he should have been the first player to exercise complete self-control."

Somehow, Mr. Horn's remarks about allowing Big Jack to give his opponent a "reprisal kick", without penalty, appear to be somewhat removed from what the laws of the game dictated, even in those days when physical contact was far less frowned upon than it is today. To his credit, Jack Charlton agreed with the referee that he should have exercised more self-control, and he indicated that he was prepared to accept his punishment without argument for what he deemed to be a single lapse.

He was fined £50, and had to pay £30 costs, at a personal hearing in front of the Football Association, and he conceded afterwards: "It was very fair; I got what I deserved." Mr. Horn wasn't so sanguine about the verdict, however. "I thought Charlton got off lightly. I am shocked and angered. Mr. Charlton is a very lucky man."

In its wisdom, the FA commission decided that Jack had acted under extreme provocation, although he was still censured and warned about his conduct in the future.

Leo Horn didn't clash only with the FA and its verdict, he had words with Leeds manager Don Revie at the time the incident happened. He claimed Revie had pleaded with him not to give Charlton marching orders and had told the manager: "Do you think this is the first time I have refereed a game?" He said Revie had pointed out that the centre-half was an international, and had answered that by retorting: "I don't care if Charlton is an emperor, he is not coming back on the field tonight."

As to the referee's talk about money, Revie said his players were not on a special bonus, and that Horn was either guessing or had been misinformed. Revie declared: "I resent these allegations, but I'm saying no more now; it's time for the whole thing to simmer down."

The newspapers suggested that both Leeds and Valencia might be barred from taking part in the Inter-Cities Fairs Cup tournament in the future, but in any event, as matters stood the teams had to meet again two weeks later in Spain. This time, Leo Horn was conspicuous by his absence. A Swiss referee and two linesmen of the same nationality were named for the match, and Leeds had the last laugh as they won through to reach the quarter-finals.

Furthermore, there was no trouble during the game, and Revie afterwards rated the Leeds display "our greatest triumph in Europe. Better, even, than our match in Turin, when we lost Bobby Collins, who suffered a broken thigh bone. There seems to be no end to the courage of my players."

When Leeds met another Spanish team, Real Zaragoza, in the semi-finals, Johnny Giles was sent off, four minutes from the final whistle, though his team-mates reckoned he was more sinned-against than sinning, since he had been chopped down in the first minute, then grabbed by the neck and struck in the kidneys.

Real Zaragoza finally managed a goal when Bremner blocked a scoring effort on the line - he had used his elbow to stop the ball going into the net - and so the Spaniards were awarded a spot-kick, which Sprake almost managed to save. In the return match at Elland Road, it was Giles who provided Jack Charlton with the chance to ram the ball past the Zaragoza 'keeper, and then, when Real scored a second-half stunner, Big Jack deserted his defensive role to move up to centre-forward.

Three minutes later, the tactic had paid off, as Norman Hunter, another defensive player turned attacker, floated over a cross which Charlton headed past 'keeper Giocoechea to make the final aggregate score 2-2. This meant that the tie had to be decided on the flip of a red-and-blue disc, so Jack and the Real skipper, Lapetra, got together in the centre circle as 45,000 fans and the rest of the players waited and held their breath.

Jack was wearing Don Revie's raincoat over his jersey, and he had the advantage of being able to call, if it could be termed an advantage, in such a lottery. He managed to get the word out: "Blue." Then his manager was hugging him and yelling: "You've done it!" Winning the toss meant that the play-off would take place at Elland Road.

Unwittingly, by making that winning call, Jack Charlton had started another rumpus, because England manager Alf Ramsey wanted both him and Norman Hunter for an international against Yugoslavia only a day or so after the date scheduled for the play-off. Finally the Fairs Cup committee agreed that the play-off could take place a week later than originally planned. Then Real Zaragoza took a hand in the proceedings.

They claimed they had chartered an aircraft for the original date, and it seemed as if they were determined to appear in Leeds on that date. It was even suggested if Leeds refused to turn out on the original date, the Spaniards might claim victory by default. And when Don Revie was asked what would happen should Real Zaragoza arrive for the match on that first date, he gave a terse, four-word reply: "We won't be there." In the end, the play-off took place on the later date, but although Jack Charlton was a marksman again, the Spaniards dazzled to score an emphatic victory and go through to the final.

There were other moments in Jack Charlton's playing career when things did not run so smoothly for him and for Leeds. For instance, a game at Elland Road against Preston North End. The match ended in a draw, but not before the referee, Eric Jennings, had stopped play in order to call the players of both sides together and give them a talking-to about the way they were going about their business.

There was an occasion when Leeds United "copped it" from the Football Association, with a report which publicised the fact that Don Revie's men had been handed more cautions (18) than any other League side during the previous term. And then there was a game against Everton at Goodison Park when Jack Charlton was the victim of an early foul, and things went from bad to worse.

Only minutes after the foul on Charlton, Johnny Giles was on the receiving end, and Everton defender Sandy Brown - normally regarded as a fair player - was given his marching orders. Then, when Willie Bell managed to score and put Leeds in front, the mood of the home supporters became even more inflamed and inflammatory.

Ten minutes before half-time there came the spark which set the tinder-box alight, as Bell and Everton forward Derek Temple embarked on a collision course by the touchline. That incident had the fans in uproar, and referee Roger Stokes decided there was nothing else for it: both teams had to go off the park. It was a history-making decision, but the referee clearly felt there was no other way, if he was to get a grip on the game.

Ironically, this match had signalled the return of Bobby Collins to Goodison Park for a League game - his first visit since his transfer to Leeds more than two years previously - and the wee man recalled that the proceedings became "nasty and brutal." While both teams were back in the dressing-room, referee Stokes was laying down the law to them, as he visited each side in turn and warned that if they didn't stop kicking lumps out of each other they would be reported to the Football Association. His parting shot was: "Start playing football."

Ten minutes later, the players returned to restart the action, and as play got under way the Goodison pitch became littered with cushions and other objects thrown by irate fans.

Despite the referee's stern admonishment to the two sides before hostilities had been resumed, he still hadn't finished with the need to reach for his notebook, and the name of Norman Hunter went into it before the final whistle had sounded, by which time no fewer than 32 fouls had been signalled.

One referee who stood no nonsense during his time on the League list was Peter Rhodes, who came from York. He was to quit refereeing in this country and join the exodus to the United States when soccer first got off the ground there, but during his time as the man in the middle for English League matches he made his own presence felt as he dismissed players and reported back-room men such as Malcolm Allison to the Football Association.

It was Rhodes who also reported Leeds manager Don Revie, after Revie had criticised referee Ray Tinkler. Rhodes reckoned that Revie should have made his feelings known not publicly but privately to the soccer authorities, and he called on the Football Association to take action.

When it came to his own players, Don Revie was always their champion, even while he was giving people like Billy Bremner and Jack Charlton a telling-off for causing problems. Indeed, Revie stood firm and stuck up for Charlton not long after the big fellow had returned from the World Cup in 1966 and lost some of the form which had earned him his England caps.

Some of the Leeds United fans, forgetting, or so it seemed, the part Big Jack had played in the club's run of success, made him a target for abuse, and one so-called supporter actually took the trouble to make a telephone call to Don Revie and issue this warning to him: "If you don't drop Jack Charlton, I'll shoot you!" It seems doubtful if the fellow ever meant what he said and, in any event, Jack Charlton regained his form, so that was the end of that.

At another stage during his career with Leeds, it appeared as if it might even be the end of Jack Charlton's career, this time not through loss of form, but through loss of fitness. Ligament trouble put him out of the game for several months, and as he began a long and tedious battle to regain his fitness, at the back of his mind there began to lurk a genuine fear that he might not have a future any longer as a top-class footballer.

When the experts were consulted, there seemed to be a difference of opinion. One medical adviser suggested that it would take an operation to provide the solution to the problem, while another advocated that weight exercises would do the trick, but Jack would have to devote a great deal of time and concentration to the job of getting fit again.

In between these two different sets of advice there came the real shaker: the knowledge that Jack wasn't the only person to be thinking and worrying whether he still had a future as a player. From inside the club came the assurance that if he found he wasn't up to resuming his playing career, then there would be a job for him at Leeds United.

In one way, of course, that assurance was something of a comfort, but in another way it added to the worry. Suddenly, it came home to Jack Charlton that his career WAS in jeopardy, so he set about trying to repair the damage by undertaking the weight exercises which had been recommended by one of his advisers. There had been a great deal of muscle wastage - almost an inch and a half had done the disappearing trick - and it took Jack all his time and patience to get through a 16-week slog involving the weight exercises.

At long last, however, the medical verdict was to his satisfaction. Indeed, not only had he regained full fitness, but as the muscle had been built up once more, he had even managed to add quarter of an inch to it. And by the time he did hang up his boots as a player with Leeds United, he had become the club's record holder for League appearances, having totalled 629. In the process, also, he had learned quite a lot about the game and about himself over a career which spanned the best part of 20 years.

He had come back after loss of form and serious injury; he had known the disappointment of being a member of the Leeds United team which, at one stage, had seemed doomed always to finish as runners-up; he had also savoured the heady delight of being in a trophy-winning side, both at club and international level. And he had overcome other obstacles - some put there by himself - to emerge as a stronger and better-balanced character who no longer carried a chip on his shoulder.

In short, and not to put too fine a point upon it, Jack Charlton had passed the ultimate test, and when he pondered upon where he should go from Elland Road, it seemed only natural that his thoughts should turn to management, even though he had once said that, after playing, he didn't feel coaching or managing a team would ever produce the same kind of satisfaction.

He did have what might be termed a sideline: a gents' outfitting business, but deep down Jack Charlton knew that after all his years in the game, and with all the experience he had gained from professional football, and the people in it, this had become a way of life for him. Other people clearly felt, too, that he was well suited to move into management, and it wasn't long before he was given the opportunity to do so and see just what he could make of the job.

Playing For Alf

Like Jack Charlton, England team-manager Sir Alf Ramsey was his own man. At a time when Jack was coming in for some criticism about his performances, his international team boss was at some pains to let him know that he still had every faith in him, and, as it turned out, that faith was justified.

Ramsey had been a cultured full-back who enjoyed success with Tottenham Hotspur and, surprisingly, as a centre-forward with Southampton, while as a manager he guided unfashionable Ipswich Town to the League championship in 1962. Then he became manager of the England international team, and during the 1966 World Cup he made headline news, not only because he steered England to ultimate triumph, either.

Many people doubted his assertion that England WOULD win the World Cup, even though they were favoured by playing all their matches on home ground. Then there was the business of Rattin's sending-off, when England met Argentina, and Ramsey made a reference to "animals." There was also controversy about his team selection: should Jimmy Greaves have been in or out? And about the formation, which gave the media cause to refer to England as "the wingless wonders."

At a later date, I travelled to London to interview the great man. By then he had been knighted, and as he talked in those clipped tones, I listened. Then I ventured a question: when it came to the World Cup, did he pick the players to suit the tactics he wished to employ, or did he make the tactics fit the players? He looked at me as if to suggest that I'd asked a damn-fool question which didn't even deserve an answer. And so we passed on to something else.

Ramsey knew his football all right: he had played for England in the 1950 World Cup, and he won 31 caps. When he graduated to management of the England side, he knew what he wanted, and he got it. More than anything, perhaps, he gained the confidence of all his players in full measure, and two of those players, Jack and

Bobby Charlton, made some kind of history as they figured in the side which won the coveted World Cup trophy.

It was on March 31, 1965, that Leeds United met, and mastered, Manchester United in the semi-finals of the FA Cup, a replay which took place on the City Ground of Nottingham Forest. That was the day, also, on which Jack Charlton learned that he had been chosen by Ramsey to play for England against Scotland at Wembley, where Leeds would be meeting Liverpool in the FA Cup final.

The word was almost literally whispered in Jack's ear in advance of the team being officially announced, so "keep it quiet" was the order of the day. But Jack couldn't resist telling brother Bobby. After all, they would switch from being rivals to teammates, and this would be the first time in a century that brothers had been picked to play in a full international (the Comptons, Denis and Leslie, had played for England, but that was during wartime).

To add spice to the occasion, Scotland had recalled Leeds inside-forward Bobby Collins after an absence of six years, while Billy Bremner was named as reserve for Scotland. Joining Jack Charlton as an England debutant was a little tough guy from Manchester United by the name of Nobby Stiles. Nobody realised it just then, but Ramsey's World Cup side was taking shape to such an extent that the entire defence which turned out against the Scots also did duty throughout the World Cup tournament. It consisted of Leicester City 'keeper Gordon Banks; right-back George Cohen, from Fulham; left-back Ramon Wilson, of Everton; centre-half Jack Charlton, and wing-halves Nobby Stiles and Bobby Moore, from West Ham.

Of the other players in the side, Bobby Charlton was also to earn undying fame in the World Cup, while Jimmy Greaves was to make a brief appearance on that stage. One critic at the time questioned Moore's presence against Scotland on the grounds that "he has not recovered the form which made him an automatic choice before his enforced lay-off." Moore was to make all his critics eat their words as he went up the steps at Wembley in 1966 to collect the World Cup.

In the match against the Scots, Ray Wilson and Johnny Byrne became injury victims, and the blue shirts swept forward to give the England defence a really testing time. Jack Charlton played a part in the goal - scored by "wor Bobby" - which put Ramsey's team ahead, then Bobby provided a chance for Greaves to make it 2-0. In reply Bobby Collins back-heeled a pass which Dennis Law rattled past Banks from all of 30 yards.

With Wilson and Byrne out of action, Bobby Charlton played at left-back in the second half, and as the Scots applied intensive pressure, it became obvious that something had to give. It did when Ian St. John nodded home a second goal for Scotland, so the result at the final whistle was 2-2.

By the time the World Cup was on the horizon, Jack Charlton, like brother Bobby, was established in the England side; and when Alf Ramsey got his men together at Lilleshall, he didn't beat about the bush. They were there to prepare for, and to win, the World Cup. Ramsey's right-hand man was Harold Shepherdson, and "Shep" followed his instructions and kept a strict check on the fitness of the players. Nothing was to be left to chance - shades of the Revie regime at Leeds United.

Some folk claimed that England's pre-World Cup tour wasn't the best way of preparing for the tournament, and the last match of the tour, which would be in Poland, was rated a very dicey affair. There were to be four games in ten days, kicking off with a gentle encounter with Finland in Helsinki. That match was won 3-0.

Next, it was on to Norway and Oslo, where England clocked up a 6-1 success; then the Danes went down 2-0 in Copenhagen; and so to Poland, who had given the Scots a beating at Hampden Park in the qualifying rounds. I was at Hampden to see that game, and Poland didn't look a bad side at all.

When they came up against England, they had an audience of 120,000 fans, but at the end of 90 minutes the home spectators had been silenced, as Roger Hunt produced a single-goal match-winner. Those Polish fans admitted that England would prove formidable opposition on their own patch, after having won four games, with a dozen goals scored and only one conceded.

The England supporters, it seemed, were not quite so optimistic about their team's chances of going all the way and up the steps to the royal box to collect the Jules Rimet trophy, and the critics came alive again after the opening match of the tournament, when England played Uruguay, who made it crystal-clear that they intended to defend, rather than go for outright victory. After ninety minutes, neither side had managed a goal, and questions were being asked.

Alf Ramsey's verdict, when he got the players back in the dressing-room, was short and very much to the point. If England hadn't won, neither had they lost, and they hadn't conceded a goal, either. His theme was that if the team continued to keep a clean sheet, they wouldn't be beaten, and they WOULD qualify. And so England went out to do battle with their next opponents, from Mexico.

The Mexicans had kept England out for the first half-hour, then Bobby Charlton broke the deadlock with a goal which his big brother afterwards rated the best England achieved during the whole tournament, and remember Geoff Hurst struck a hat-trick in the final.

Bobby collected the ball in his own half, and with Nobby Stiles making a break the Mexicans clearly expected him to receive a pass. Instead, Bobby kept right on going, while the opposition retreated and waited for the pass to be made. Yet still Bobby Charlton, jinking one way and then the other, drove forward - then he let fly with a rocket-like shot which left the Mexican goalkeeper, Calderon, clawing at air as he dived. The ball was already nestling in the net behind him.

When Roger Hunt got his name on the scoresheet, with quarter of an hour remaining, Mexico surrendered, and England had three points out of four. Suddenly, the critics were viewing the scene in a somewhat different light.

As in 1994, so it was in 1966 that players were picked out to undergo dope tests. In 1994 Maradona was banished after a test proved positive, and in 1966 Jack Charlton was the man picked out to take the dope test after the match against Mexico. Sometimes, players find that they can't oblige - that happened more than once during the World Cup tournament in the United States - and the testers have to wait awhile. Jack Charlton managed to provide a sample on demand, however, and there were no problems for him.

Now it was France who barred the way, and they needed to win if they were to have a chance of going through to the quarter-finals, so they were the team under most pressure at this stage. Roger Hunt demonstrated that Alf Ramsey had been right to pick him, despite the fact that some people labelled him a "work-horse." Against France, he scored the two goals which carried England into the quarter-finals, with a record of five points out of six, four goals scored in three matches, and none conceded.

The next match promised to be intriguing, because it was against South American opposition, Argentina. For this one, there was a German referee named Rudolf Kreitlein, and before the day was over he was to be making headline news, along with Antonio Rattin, Argentina's captain.

Argentina had already achieved a status of some notoriety by becoming the first team to have had a player sent off (the player in question was Albrecht), and now Herr Kreitlein, bald-headed, not too significant in stature, but certainly too fussy from Argentina's point of view, demonstrated that if he were no giant, neither was he prepared to tolerate any funny business.

The South Americans indulged in some tricks which were not in the book of rules. They aroused the ire of the England supporters and players, and they attracted the constant attention of referee Kreitlein, who seemed not only to be constantly whistling for infringements, but to be noting down the names of one Argentine player after another.

Argentina committed what one observer called "the calculated foul" time and again, and for one of these Rattin was booked. His victim was Bobby Charlton. There came a moment when, yet again, as captain he objected to the booking of another team-mate, and Herr Kreitlein had decided that enough was enough. His arm went up, and he signalled the end of the game for Senor Rattin.

There was only one snag: Rattin simply refused to go. When he found himself being banished, he remained on the touchline, while team-manager Lorenzo appeared and team-mates went to join in a conference with him. They remonstrated not only with referee Kreitlein, but with Ken Aston, the head of the Referees' Committee, while Harry Cavan, the FIFA commissaire for the game, also went on the pitch to try to restore some semblance of order.

While the fans sang "Why are we waiting?", the confrontations on the pitch continued, and at one stage it seemed that the whole of the Argentinian team was prepared to stage a World Cup walk-out. Ten minutes had passed before Senor Rattin finally decided to obey the referee's injunction to walk away from the proceedings (he was still gesturing his dismay and his innocence), and at the final whistle - after a Geoff Hurst headed goal had taken England into the semi-finals - police had to ensure that Herr Kreitlein came to no harm from Argentinians who appeared likely to wreak vengeance upon him.

The next morning the Sunday papers published pictures of the amazing scenes at Wembley, and later there was one of referee Kreitlein enjoying a peaceful stroll in a London park. Meanwhile, England were raring to go against Portugal, who had come through their Goodison Park tussle with unrated North Korea to claim their place in the semi-finals.

I was at Goodison Park for one of the most absorbing, entertaining and astonishing matches of the tournament, because the so-called no-hopers from North Korea almost stood the World Cup on its head. My report of the match began: "Eusebio has taken over the mantle of the great from Pélé. Portugal can thank their ace and his four goals (two from penalties) for preventing the shock result of the World Cup."

Pélé and his Brazilian team-mates discovered that the 1966 World Cup was far from being a joy-ride: they were beset by injury problems and it was claimed by some that they were, indeed, kicked out of the tournament by opponents who were not too fussy as to how they achieved their victories. I had seen Portugal end Brazil's eight-year reign as world champions when they won 3-1 at Goodison. In that match Brazil lost Pélé through injury with only half an hour gone.

Brazil had made several surprising changes, and Portugal were two up when Pélé - who had survived some tough tackles before his injury - retired from the action, and even though he tried to make a comeback he was, in essence, little more than a cripple. The collision with Morais sounded the death-knell of Brazil's hopes. Pélé was carried off, then five minutes later he was back, but limping. In the second half he remained on the field but, with his right knee heavily bandaged, he was no more than a passenger.

So the Portuguese returned to Goodison to take on the North Koreans, and for the assembled Press corps there were problems enough in getting round the tongue-twisting names of the little men from the Far East. Try pronouncing Pak Seung Zin, Li Dong Woon, Yang Sung Kook, among others, when you're on the end of a telephone and the copy-taker at the other end is asking you: "What did you say?" And all this amid the roar of the crowd!

At any rate, this match, which most people regarded as a formality for Portugal, turned into a sizzling drama as the North Koreans raced into a three-goal lead inside the first half-hour. The

Portuguese found themselves a goal down in 60 seconds, and not until they had surrendered two more goals did they get to grips with the task which confronted them.

The fight-back began with a goal from - who else? - Eusebio, and when the giant striker Torres went down inside the penalty area, Eusebio made it 3-2 from the spot. Shortly after half-time, the writing was on the wall for the North Koreans as Eusebio snapped up a pass from Simoes and made it a hat-trick when he scored with an angled drive.

If the North Koreans never gave up - and twice they had the Portuguese defence in a tangle - they were now doomed to finish as losers. Eusebio wove a way into their penalty area, leaving two opponents stranded, and after he had been stopped by the simple expedient of bringing him down, he shrugged aside an apparent injury to a leg, strode up and side-footed the spot-kick into the net. For the first time Portugal were ahead, two goals in as many minutes giving them the edge. They were through to a semi-final contest with Alf Ramsey's England.

Meanwhile, as England celebrated their narrow victory over Argentina, the Charlton brothers were somewhat taken aback to learn from manager Alf Ramsey that apart from the bookings and the sending-off of Senor Rattin, they might be heading for trouble. Seemingly, they had been reported to football's governing body, FIFA, and accused of ungentlemanly conduct. As it turned out, the matter appeared to die a death, and the brothers were able to take their places in the line-up against the Portuguese.

This was the game which, according to Cissie Charlton, "should have been the final", and certainly it was played in an inspiring and sporting atmosphere, totally different from that of the encounter with Argentina. A Frenchman, Pierre Schwinte, was given the job of handling the semi-final, with linesmen from Peru and Yugoslavia to assist him.

The duel was described by one writer as being "a match as satisfying and sporting as any ever seen on an international field", and it was recorded also that England "set a defence to shut out the magnificent Portuguese and won the victory with two typical goals of class from Bobby Charlton."

What about Big Jack? He set the supporters buzzing, too, by giving away a penalty! So the match then was balanced so finely that anything could have happened once Eusebio had sent 'keeper

Gordon Banks the wrong way with the spot-kick. At that stage of the game there remained only eight minutes on the clock, but for Jack Charlton, his team-mates and the England supporters they were eight extremely long minutes. This was the first goal which England had conceded in the World Cup competition.

The semi-final was in stark contrast to some of the matches which had gone before. It was said that the whole tournament, up to then, had been "marred by chauvinistic dissension, nastiness and ill-feeling", yet when England and Portugal met, almost half an hour had passed before the referee felt it necessary to award a free-kick, while play had been going for close on an hour before a foul was committed on an England player.

If England had a rock-solid defence, with Jack Charlton a major player, the Portuguese had a scintillating attack. Charlton and Moore, it was recorded, were composed and safe in the best defence in the world, while full-backs Cohen and Wilson were never mastered. And these four stalwarts, in front of Gordon Banks, were backed up by the non-stop efforts of Nobby Stiles.

Admiration was also expressed for "that thoroughbred of a player Bobby Charlton", who produced some telling passes from midfield and proceeded to add lustre to his display by scoring "two historic goals", after Geoff Hurst and Roger Hunt had gone close, as they went at a vulnerable Portuguese defence.

Half an hour had gone by when Bobby Charlton struck for the first time. The ball was whipped through by Ray Wilson, and though Hunt gave chase he couldn't manage to gain control. However, his darting run was sufficient to fluster the 'keeper, who raced from his line, then slid a yard or so, and appeared to divert the ball away with the soles of his boots.

The 'keeper hadn't got away with it, though - the ball ran straight to Bobby Charlton, who didn't hesitate to make the most of his chance. He latched on to the ball and, using the inside of his foot, drove his shot into the middle of the gaping goal. England were ahead.

The Portuguese, far from hanging their heads, reacted by stepping up the pace. A tremendous shot from Eusebio was held by Banks at the second attempt, and a drive from Torres scraped past an upright. In the second half Jack Charlton and Moore, aided and abetted by Stiles, coped with everything Portugal could throw at them, and with Torres rising to the occasion, and Coluna and

Simoes sparking attacks, there was plenty of work to be done.

After 57 minutes Portugal conceded their first foul, when Coluna obstructed Moore, but this was no more than a mere hiccup in a game of ebb-and-flow. Portugal found their best efforts were foundering on England's rock-like defence, but at 1-0 there was still everything to play for. Eleven minutes from the end, however, England struck again.

The home side broke clear, with Hurst going down the right flank and Bobby Charlton racing through the middle. Hurst judged his pass to perfection as he stroked the ball towards his team-mate, and Bobby took it in his stride, then struck the ball perfectly, to register another spectacular goal. The fans then believed it was all over bar the shouting, and they were calling out: "We want three!" But it wasn't quite over yet.

Torres, who had always threatened danger - notably in the air - won an aerial duel and headed the ball to the unmarked Eusebio. Before it could reach him, however, Jack Charlton intervened. Having spotted the danger, he punched the ball clear, and that, as he knew immediately, meant a penalty. So a hush descended upon the stadium as almost 100,000 people waited to see if Portugal would score.

The man deputed to take the penalty was Eusebio, and he had the right temperament for such a nerve-wracking occasion. As Jack Charlton was seen to be holding his head in his hands, afraid to watch what happened next, Eusebio sent the England 'keeper diving the wrong way. After this goal, Portugal gave England another scare when Coluna unleashed a thundering drive which Banks managed to tip over the bar. But, at last, the semi-final was over and England had triumphed.

For Eusebio and his team-mates, it was the end of the World Cup road, and as he was led off the pitch, the cameras captured a moment of emotion, as he lifted his jersey and wiped away his tears. There were tears, too, from the England players - tears of joy, and it was recorded that "Big Jack Charlton, the strong man of the greatest defence on earth, wept with them. He was embraced by his brother Bobby, arguably the greatest forward in the game, and as this pair walked off along with the other England players, there was a final roar from the raw and tortured throats of the finest fan club that ever inspired an England side."

So wrote Desmond Hackett in the Daily Express, and in Jack

Charlton's case, he was to experience a similar reception from a different fan club: the Irishmen who cheered on their side in the 1994 World Cup, with 100,000 of them giving Big Jack and his boys a rousing welcome home on their arrival at Dublin's Phoenix Park. Back in 1966, however, Jack had no inkling of what the future would hold for him. Right there and then, he and brother Bobby were just content to enjoy the knowledge that they would be taking part in the final of the World Cup.

June 22nd 1966 - Jack with Jimmy Armfield and Nobby Stiles.

July 11th 1966
- Ladislao Mazurk-Ieviez,
the Uruguyan goalkeeper,
gets to the ball before Jack
in the opening match
of the World Cup.
Result was a goalless draw,
even though Jimmy Greaves
awaits his chance.

July 16th 1966 - Ignacio Calderon punches away from the ever
dangerous Jack. England beat Mexico 2-0.

July 29th 1966 - Bobby's wife Norma with parents-in-law Bob and
Cissie - "How will our boys play tomorrow in the final?"

30th July 1966 - The World Cup final line-up at Wembley - Jack's at
the end of the line.

30th July 1966 - Alf Ramsey doesn't look all that happy as he discusses the match with Prime Minister Harold Wilson. Former referee, Denis Howell, Minister for Sport, listens in.

30th July 1966 - Lucky dad Bob plays host to the wives and girlfriends of the England squad.

November 1993 and Jack doesn't like what's happening out there.

5th June 1994 and a few kind words from a fan after the Czechs beat Eire in Dublin by three goals to one.

14th January 1992 and brother Bobby acknowledges the as yet
unnamed mascot for England.

(No pictures of the mascot being buried are available!)

28th June 1993 - Jack and wife Pat say their fond farewells to Bobby Moore at Westminster Abbey.

It's December 1993 and Jack smiles as he hears the draw for the
World Cup at the American Embassy in Dublin.

No he doesn't! Alarm...
It's Italy, Mexico, Norway.

"Never mind the ball - here's the new kit lads!" Training in America, June 1994.

Never mind the football, what about the sights?
The full squad visit the Universal Studios in Florida.

Yabba-Dabba-Do! Roy Keane with some of the Flintstone characters.

"Mine for yours," an Irish fan offers, but Jack's not taking anything off - Orlando training ground, 7th June 1994.

When in Rome... the end of all the talking and the training. Now it's the real thing - Meadowland ground, 17th June 1994.

"Pure genius - and good thinking Andy," but it wasn't to be.

The Republic of Ireland's fans celebrate the goal that beats Italy - New Jersey, 18th June 1994.

18th June and eventual finalists Italy have lost by one goal to nil, scored by Houghton and celebrated by the manager and his team.

Jack feels the air and prefers ballet at the Orlando Citrus Bowl.

Jack's happy! And why not, his team have held Norway to a goalless draw at the Giant's stadium in New Jersey, 28th June 1994.

"And you know what you can do with that camera - these tactics are confidential," suggests Jack.

"Leave it out Boss," - Andy Townsend appeals during a training session in Orlando.

Jack smiles and hugs Dick Advocaat, but it's the end for Eire after losing 2-0 to the Dutchmen, 4th July 1994.

A disappointed Jack arrives home from the World Cup, defeated but not vanquished, accompanied by Albert Reynolds and Dick Spring.

World Cup Winners

It was the gap-toothed, grinning Nobby Stiles who so aptly summed up the feelings of every England player when, after the World Cup final of 1966, he danced a victory jig at Wembley and declared: "Nobody can take this away from us." Nobby, along with the Charlton brothers and their team-mates, had walked up the steps to the royal box at Wembley and received from the Queen the little gold medal that said everything.

It was July 30, 1966, and while Cissie Charlton and her husband were down in London for the World Cup final, Mrs Pat Charlton - Jack's wife - was at home in Leeds, expecting a baby. As if Big Jack hadn't enough on his mind, wondering when the baby would be born, he was about to take part in the World Cup final. As the time drew closer, he and the rest of the England players trooped into the private room where team-manager Alf Ramsey would give them their briefing on the game against West Germany.

People in football are often superstitious: Don Revie, during his days as Leeds United's manager, had a "lucky" blue suit, while by the time the World Cup had come round, two Leeds team mates - Norman Hunter and Jack Charlton - had a pre-match routine when they were on England duty. Each of them occupied the same two seats on the team coach as it took them to Wembley stadium.

There, once the players had got changed, they walked out to line up with their West German rivals, then proceeded to the pitch to the accompaniment of a thunderous roar from almost 100,000 partisan spectators. The scene was set for the final battle.

The parents of the Charlton brothers had been invited down for the final, and like the thousands of other people packed into the ground, they were willing their favourites to win. For them, it was an intensely personal occasion, since two of their four sons were appearing on the World Cup stage. And they saw Jack and Bobby savour the taste of victory, but only after one or two alarms along the way.

It was indeed a final of high drama, and hearts were in mouths as early as the 13th minute, when the England players found themselves a goal behind. For once, England's much-vaunted defence was caught napping, as Siggi Held steered a high cross from the left wing and Wilson, untroubled by any opponent, rose to head clear. Instead, he saw the ball dropping down to the feet of Helmut Haller, who was standing no more than a dozen yards from goal.

Haller had all the time in the world, right at the moment the ball was delivered to his feet - time to steady himself, time to pivot and direct a right-foot daisy-cutter past the right side of 'keeper Gordon Banks. But if the Germans thought they were on their way to a victory, they had reason to think again, little more than five minutes later.

After having been given a talking-to for a foul on Alan Ball, Wolfgang Overath committed another indiscretion as he tripped England skipper Bobby Moore. The free-kick was given, and Moore himself took it, from 40 yards out near the left touchline. This accomplished footballer flighted the free-kick towards the far post and Geoff Hurst timed his run precisely as he drifted through the German defence then struck a scoring header low inside the right-hand post of 'keeper Hans Tilkowski.

When Bobby Charlton made a run, he finished off with a left-footer which Tilkowski managed to smother at the second attempt, then it was the turn of Banks to beat Haller in a race for possession at the other end of the field. At this point England were giving at least as good as they got, although it was said that they needed Bobby Charlton to be in two places at once: he was providing the ammunition from midfield, but England could also have done with him to be finishing off such moves, from a front-line position.

Yet another England goal almost came, when Hurst put in a goalbound header. Tilkowski scrambled the ball away, only to see Ball turn it back into the goalmouth, where a desperate Overath whacked it away for a corner. At the other end, it was Jack Charlton to the rescue as Held threatened danger near the by-line. While Ball and Cohen jockeyed the German, it was left to Big Jack to come in with a sweeping tackle and whip the ball away, even though it meant conceding a corner.

Jack's heart was in his mouth, though, when the corner kick came over, for it almost led to a second German goal. The ball went to Overath, some 20 yards distant, and straight away he hammered in a fierce drive, chest-high. Banks couldn't hold the ball, he beat it out, then managed to make the catch as Lothar "Big Bertha" Emmerich rammed in a shot from an acute angle. Emmerich was nicknamed "Big Bertha" after a famous German gun of the First World War which had tremendous firing power.

As England attacked, Wilson's header into goal was nodded down by Hurst, and Hunt forced the ball goalwards, only to see this effort blocked by the 'keeper, while shortly before half-time the cat-and-mouse aspect of the final was emphasised yet again as the Germans went close, with Banks brilliantly turning a vicious 20-yard drive from Overath over the bar.

In the second half, Willie Schulz brought down Bobby Charlton, but the fans' appeal for a penalty was no more than a muted cry. Then Hunt was crowded out as he tried to get on the end of a cross from the left, but this was simply the prelude to another England goal.

There were 15 minutes of the match remaining when Hunt delivered a pass to Ball, who shot for goal. Tilkowski pushed the shot away for a corner, and when this was taken, Hurst shot from the left. Schulz deflected this effort right across the face of the goal, and Martin Peters, so adept at ghosting into a scoring position, deceived the German defence as he moved in quickly to catch the ball on the half-volley and ram it home from only a few yards. England 2, West Germany 1, and the scent of World Cup victory was in the air.

Two other players were upfield when Peters struck that goal, one of them was Jack Charlton, and the chance might so easily have fallen to him. As it was, he played a major role in the goal which West Germany scored during the dying seconds of the final. As he had done so often before when the ball came through the air into the danger area, Charlton rose to the occasion, but as he went to head the ball clear referee Gottfried Dienst, who had officiated in a somewhat fussy style, decided that West Germany should be awarded a free-kick.

You could almost have heard a pin drop as Lothar Emmerich prepared to take the free-kick, then drove the ball through the defensive wall set up by the England players. Some said the ball was handled by Karl-Heinz Schnellinger; some said Helmut Haller was the man who handled it. Whatever, referee Dienst this time saw nothing wrong with what happened, and the ball travelled on to Weber, who gratefully stuck the scoring chance away as he lurked by the far post.

Jack Charlton and his team-mates were all but shattered as they sank to the turf and massaged tired limbs while waiting for extra time to begin. Their manager moved them, telling them to get cracking again, and the gist of his message was: "You've won the World Cup once - now go and win it again." At that precise moment, of course, it was easier said than done, but the players picked themselves up and started to respond.

Once again, it was England in the ascendancy as the first period of extra time got under way, and they swept forward into the German penalty area, with Ball - working even more energetically than he had done during the previous 90 minutes - hammering in a shot from 20 yards which appeared to have "Goal" written all over it, until Tilkowski somehow managed to tip the ball over the bar. Then it was Bobby Charlton's turn to suffer, as the West German 'keeper pushed a drive against a post, and saw the ball rebound to safety.

When the Germans attacked, Stiles came to the rescue, then Held really made the England supporters hold their breath as he jinked his way clear of the entire defence and cut the ball back across the face of goal, but there wasn't a German team-mate there to cash in on this tantalising opportunity. And then, in the tenth minute of extra time, England scored a goal which was argued about for years.

Ball, bustling down the right side of the field, created an opening, and the ball went in to Hurst, who pushed forward until he could see the German goalmouth ahead. Then he struck a right-foot shot on the turn, some 10 yards out, and as Tilkowski went for it, he pushed the ball upwards, so that it crashed against the under-side of the bar, before bouncing down again.

Roger Hunt, who had been an interested spectator of all this, to say the least, immediately turned away with his arm raised, signalling a goal; and his team-mates all joined in this clear appeal which claimed that the ball, having bounced down from the bar, had indeed crossed the line. Referee Dienst remained to be convinced, however. He made his way across to the Russian linesman and there was a consultation while everyone in the stadium waited with baited breath! When the referee's verdict came, there was a roar from the England fans, while the players danced with delight - it was, after all, a goal.

The West Germans, having salvaged extra time with their controversial, last-gasp equaliser, were stunned, and unable to get to grips with things again. Both sides, indeed, were flagging, and players had their socks rolled down as the minutes dragged by. England were hanging on to their precious, single-goal lead, and the end of the match was looming Then it really was all over, even though the final whistle had not been blown.

One more attack from England, one more effort from marksman Hurst, one more pass from skipper Moore. As Hurst took the ball and staggered more than strode, he summoned up the strength to hit the ball into the roof of the German net and make the scoreline England 4, West Germany 2. This time, not even the Germans could stage a comeback, and as the realisation that the World Cup had been won dawned on the home players, Bobby Charlton was not the only one to shed a tear, while Big Jack, down on his knees on the Wembley turf, his hands held to his head, admitted later: "I didn't know whether to laugh or to cry."

That had been the first World Cup final to go to extra time since 1934, when Italy had defeated Czechoslovakia in Rome. And while it was thus not the only final to have required more than 90 minutes to settle it, it was generally agreed that there had never been a final of greater drama.

The 1966 World Cup triumph, however, put England's team manager and his players under even greater pressure, as the supporters viewed the 1968 European championships and the 1970 World Cup in Mexico. In April, 1967, a cautionary note was struck when Scotland beat England 3-2 at Wembley, after Jack Charlton had been injured early on, and so was able to do little more than limp around for the remainder of the match.

England did manage to qualify for the quarter-finals of the European competition, however, and a Bobby Charlton goal helped them defeat Spain in the first leg at Wembley, while they went to Madrid and in the hostile atmosphere of the Bernabeau stadium recorded a 2-1 victory. In Florence, though, where they came up against Yugoslavia in the semi-finals, the opposition was underrated by many people, and it turned out to be a tense affair, with England losing out to a late goal. So England met Russia in the play-off for third place, and scored a 2-0 win.

By the time people's thoughts were turning to the World Cup, Ramsey's team was showing signs of change: Roger Hunt had left

Liverpool for Bolton, Alan Mullery took over from Nobby Stiles, and the years were catching up with Jack Charlton. England were grouped with Brazil, Romania and Czechoslovakia, and that didn't make things any easier, either, but the squad which left for Mexico was in high spirits.

It was while England were in Bogota, Colombia, where they had gone for a pre-World Cup match, that Bobby Moore was accused of the theft of a bracelet from a shop. It meant days of investigations, with Moore being detained, then England's skipper, still maintaining his innocence, was allowed to rejoin the squad and start thinking about playing in the World Cup, where he did himself and his country proud.

For the first match, Brian Labone partnered Moore when England met Romania, while Ball, Bobby Charlton, Peters, Banks and Hurst remained from the 1966 line-up. Hurst was the match-winner, and then it was on to a confrontation with Brazil, Pélé and all. He set up a goal for Jairzinho which won the match. Then a win over Czechoslovakia took England into the quarter-finals, and a test against their Wembley victims of 1966, West Germany.

It was in Leon that Bobby Charlton claimed his 106th international cap to set a new England record; in Leon where England let slip a 2-0 lead and had to face extra time, as they had done in 1966. Hurst, Francis Lee, Mullery and even Brian Labone all went close to scoring, but five minutes into the second period of extra time Gerd Muller drifted away from Labone, and he didn't miss from three yards. So England missed out on a semi-final place, and for the Charlton brothers, their World Cup adventure had come to an end, since Bobby's record-breaking appearance was also his last for his country.

Being "The Boss"

Leeds United finished season 1973-74 as champions of the Football League, with a total of 62 points. Liverpool were the runners-up. Leeds manager Don Revie was destined to leave Elland Road, where he had worked wonders, and become a not-very-happy manager of the England international side, but as he savoured the success of season 1973-74, one of the men who had given him both headaches and happiness through the years gone by was no longer at Leeds. Jack Charlton was making his own way as a club manager, and making a very successful job of it, too.

It has been suggested that he was never cut out to be a club manager, and that during his career as team boss at Middlesbrough, Sheffield Wednesday and Newcastle United he himself often gave indications of not being 100 per cent content in his job, that the day-to-day grind of club management conflicted with his liking for going on fishing and shooting expeditions.

While there appeared to be some rather grudging acceptance that his managerial methods were successful, on the whole critics - especially during his days at Ayresome Park and at St James' Park - were swift to claim that the teams under Big Jack's command didn't perform with genuine flair, but were functional, and simply did their job.

Functional? Middlesbrough could certainly claim to have been blessed with this quality as they emulated Leeds United in the spring of 1974, for while Leeds topped the First Division, Boro' headed the Second, champions, with 65 points, which gave them a 15-point margin over runners-up Luton Town.

By the time Middlesbrough went to play Liverpool at Anfield in the early part of October, 1974, Jack Charlton - named Manager of the Year the previous spring - had the satisfaction of also knowing that his First Division newcomers were keeping pace (well, almost) with Bill Shankly's established giants. After eleven matches, Ipswich Town led the way at the top, while Liverpool were in second place, Manchester City third, Everton fourth and Boro' fifth. Ipswich had sixteen points, Liverpool and Manchester City 15 points apiece, Everton 14 and Middlesbrough 13, but Boro' had a match in hand on each of the clubs above them.

The final League table of season 1974-75 left everyone in no doubt that Jack Charlton's team could and would survive in the top flight. Once again, Liverpool had had to settle for second place (this time out, Derby County were the League champions), and while Boro' had slipped a notch or two since they had played at Anfield in the October (where they had lost 2-0 in the League, then won 1-0 the following month in a League Cup-tie), they had contrived to finish the campaign in a very creditable seventh place.

Champions Derby wound up with 53 points, Liverpool with 51, as did Ipswich Town; then came Stoke City and Sheffield United, each with 49 points, and they were followed by Middlesbrough, on 48 points. So Boro' had been no more than five points adrift of the top spot, and they had won 18 and drawn a dozen of their 42 matches, scoring 54 goals and conceding 40.

If Big Jack didn't particularly fancy the sight of the ball going into the Boro' net 40 times over, he could reflect that during his days at Leeds United he had been a member of a defence which, in successive seasons, had leaked in no fewer than 92 goals and then 83 goals! He could also recall his first visit to Anfield - Leeds then were managed by Jack Taylor, and the Elland Road club was in the Second Division.

Leeds had kicked off the season by taking three points out of four, so they were in fairly confident mood when they went to tackle Liverpool. Shankly's team soon put paid to any feelings of complacency Leeds might have had; Liverpool stuck five goals past them. "It brought us down to earth," Jack said. "In fact, we went on to have a bad season."

Jack also remembered another occasion, when Leeds drew there to clinch the First Division championship in season 1968-69, and spoke of how on that ground "you were always under terrific pressure, under fire from the crowd. But it was always good-humoured, never vicious. That's where they started calling me 'Dirty Big Giraffe',but I never felt the Liverpool fans were antagonistic towards me. I always felt that, deep down, they liked me, and Anfield surely was my favourite away ground."

When he went back as the manager of Middlesbrough, he confessed that he knew it would be "nerve-wracking", but "if your players have character and they can play a bit, that's the place to show it. This game is all about character, and if my lads do have any flaws, this is where they'll be exposed." The 2-0 defeat said something, of course, but Boro's 1-0 League Cup triumph only a few weeks later also stated the case for Jack Charlton's influence as a team boss.

Middlesbrough kicked off season 1974-75 by going to St. Andrews and inflicting a 3-0 defeat upon Birmingham City, then they drew matches against Luton Town, Stoke City and Chelsea. After losing away against Sheffield United, they defeated Manchester City 3-0, won 2-1 away against Tottenham Hotspur, repeated that result against Wolves, then lost at Anfield.

Next came an amazing, 4-4 draw against Coventry City at Ayresome Park, where Graeme Souness (two goals), David Mills and Alan Foggon were the Boro' marksmen. Souness was later to go to Liverpool for a record £352,000, Mills to West Brom for even more: half a million pounds.

A 3-2 victory at Derby was followed by a 3-0 drubbing at West Ham's Upton Park ground and a scoreless home draw against Newcastle United. Then Jack Charlton took his team back to his old stamping ground, Elland Road, where Duncan McKenzie, a £250,000 signing by Brian Clough (once of Middlesbrough) scored twice inside five minutes, early in the first half, only to see Boro' bounce back with a goal shortly before half-time and another soon after the restart.

Boro' lost 1-3 at home against Queen's Park Rangers and 2-0 against Arsenal at Highbury, but two goals from Souness helped them defeat Ipswich Town 3-0.

They did the double over Birmingham, with a 3-0 win, and had been in the top half-dozen virtually all the time. Now they were into the second half of the season, and after losing 2-0 at Ipswich and drawing no-score with Arsenal, they hammered Sunderland 3-1 in the fourth round of the FA Cup (having first been taken to an Ayresome Park replay by Wycombe).

In the League, Boro' lost the return at Newcastle by the odd goal in three, drew no-score at home against West Ham and 1-1 in the fifth round of the FA Cup at Peterborough. An Allan Clarke goal saw Leeds home and dry in the League return at Ayresome, but after a 2-0 home victory over Stoke, Boro' bowed out of the FA Cup, beaten in round six by a Bob Hatton strike at Birmingham.

Yet they proved resilient by scoring a 3-0 home win over Spurs and going to Stamford Bridge and beating Chelsea by the odd goal in three. The character Jack Charlton had talked about was showing through. A 2-0 home win over Burnley left Middlesbrough in fourth place, with five matches to go, and a sneaking hope of lifting the First Division championship.

At the top it was Bob Paisley's Liverpool, on 45 points, then came Everton (44), Ipswich, Middlesbrough and Stoke (all bracketed on 43). But as Liverpool won 2-0 at Leeds (Kevin Keegan got the goals), Boro' had to share the points at home with Derby County, who got their equaliser in the dying seconds.

Wolves hammered another nail in the coffin as they beat Boro' 2-0 at Molineux, and though an Alan Foggon goal was the match-winner against Liverpool at Ayresome Park, the damage had already been done. With only one game to go, there was no way Boro' could close the gap between themselves and the leaders. As things turned out, Liverpool, too, lost out as Derby County claimed the title. All in all, however, Jack Charlton and his team had made their point in the First Division - nobody could take them for granted.

When Middlesbrough went back to Anfield the following season, thirty-two games had gone by, and Liverpool were leading the pack, while Boro' were in sixth place, just behind Jack Charlton's old club, Leeds United. At the end of the season, Liverpool had given manager Bob Paisley his first major prize - the League championship - while Middlesbrough, on 40 points, were finishing in a mid-table position, unlucky thirteenth.

That day at Anfield, Liverpool were looking to score their 100th goal in 46 League meetings there between the clubs, but they were shattered when Boro' forged a two-goal lead to claim the points. By then, Jack Charlton had one of England's World Cup "old boys" giving him the benefit of his experience on the backroom side at Ayresome Park, because Harold Shepherdson was the man detailed to make advanced checks on the opposition.

'Shep', the England team trainer under Sir Alf Ramsey, had been rewarded with the MBE, Charlton with the OBE. Now they were in harness together again, with Shepherdson the assistant manager at Middlesbrough. Graeme Souness was still a Boro' player, while Phil Boersma, whom he was later to take back to Anfield when he landed the manager's job there, had left Liverpool to play for Boro'.

At the beginning of October, 1976, Middlesbrough arrived at Anfield full of confidence, after having remained unbeaten until their sixth match of the campaign. Now, after seven matches, they were level on points (10) with Bob Paisley's team at the top of the First Division. Their only defeat had come about when they went to Old Trafford and lost 2-0 against 'wor Bobby's' old club, Manchester United.

Jack was saying that Saturday in October: "It makes a difference to players: they approach the game with a lot more confidence when they think back to the result they got the last time they played there." Boro' could then look back upon two victories at Anfield in recent seasons. Yet Jack Charlton wasn't blinded to the need for more firepower - "Our problem has been goals. We've been creating chances, but not taking them, and it's become a serious problem for us. It's one that's got to be solved, though."

By May, 1977, Middlesbrough had seen the gap between Liverpool and themselves widen. Paisley's men were heading for the championship again, while Boro' were in a mid-table position once more. Come January, 1978, and Liverpool and Middlesbrough were heading for 100 meetings in League games, and that particular day (Monday, January 2) the player who got his name on the scoresheet first for Liverpool would be making it 100 goals up for his club in matches against Middlesbrough at Anfield.

Jack Charlton, however, had really no more than an academic interest in the outcome of that fixture (Liverpool won, 2-0), because by then the Ayresome Park club was under new management. After four years with Boro', Big Jack had tendered his resignation and moved on, to Sheffield Wednesday, while John Neal had been appointed from Wrexham as Charlton's successor. Still at Ayresome was the man who had been No.2 to Jack, Harold Shepherdson, born no more than a stone's throw from the ground, and at one time in his footballing career a centre-half with Middlesbrough. That was in the era of "golden boy" Wilf Mannion and the debonair full-back, George Hardwick, both of whom were capped by England.

"Shep" had become trainer at Middlesbrough after the war and assistant manager in 1965. Then, for 17 years - from 1957 - he doubled up as the England trainer, under first Walter Winterbottom and then Sir Alf Ramsey. For a brief spell, even, early in 1973, he had acted as the manager at Middlesbrough, after Stan Anderson had resigned. However, he had been happy to hand over the reins to Jack Charlton and concentrate upon handling the young players and compiling dossiers on rival teams, of which Sheffield Wednesday, managed by Jack Charlton, became one.

In season 1977-78, Sheffield Wednesday were languishing in the Third Division, and Jack Charlton's mission, of course, was to do what he had done for Middlesbrough and steer them to promotion, then, hopefully, back into the top flight. After three matches, Wednesday were down the table, fifth from bottom, and after half a dozen matches they were faring even worse, next to the foot of the table, with only three points. One more game, and they had swapped places with the bottom club, Hereford United.

Wednesday were still anchored at the bottom of the Third Division with 15 matches gone, but at last they moved up one place, to leap-frog over Portsmouth. With 18 matches behind them, however, Wednesday were back again, propping up all the rest of the clubs in their division, and this remained the situation as the season passed its half-way mark and 1978 loomed ahead.

After losing 3-1 against Tranmere Rovers at Prenton Park in the last week of December, Wednesday scraped a 1-0 home win over Hereford on Monday, January 2, 1978, but the revival was brief.

With two dozen games gone, they were back on the floor, then they drew 2-2 at Swindon and won their next match, to climb five places in the table. One more victory, 3-2, at home against Bury, took them another step towards safety, and another home win, 3-1 against Port Vale, edged them further away from trouble.

It was a season when a fair number of matches were postponed, and Wednesday were one of the clubs which had to play a waiting game, but by dint of some hard-fought draws (against Portsmouth and at Chesterfield) they managed to keep their distance from the foot of the table, and a 2-1 victory over Rotherham United at Millmoor did their survival prospects a power of good. Then they defeated Tranmere Rovers 1-0 at Hillsbrough.

By then they had nine matches to go, and they were eight places from the bottom, with several points to spare on the clubs below, who were fighting desperately to stay in the Third Division. A 1-0 win at Hereford increased Wednesday's confidence that they would stay up, and with a 2-1 home win over Oxford United and two games left, safety seemed to be assured.

Despite a 2-1 defeat at Gillingham and a 0-0 home draw with Cambridge United, Wednesday remained on course, and the season came to a close with the club still members of the Third Division, although the first Saturday of the following campaign saw Wednesday going down 2-0 at Peterborough.

They picked up their first point with a home draw against Colchester United, won 2-1 at Lincoln to climb from fifth to eighth from bottom, and after having beaten Southend United by the odd goal in five at Hillsborough, they were looking upwards. There were now 10 clubs above them. Then there came a slide back down the table, after a series of draws and defeats at home against Plymouth Argyle and Walsall.

However, a 1-0 victory at Blackpool hoisted Wednesday up to 11th place, then came more draws and defeats, so that by early December they were back in the lower half of the table. The last week in December brought a 3-3 draw at Chesterfield, and after several postponements in January, Wednesday went to Plymouth and lost to Argyle for the second time during the season. They were now seventh from the foot of the Third Division.

They had played only 10 times at home in 22 outings, though, and there came another postponement when they should have met Swindon Town at Hillsborough. By then, some clubs had played 27 and 28 matches, to Wednesday's 22, so they had a fair bit of catching up to do. The home game against Rotherham was called off, but at last Wednesday's season got under way again, and after a draw at Brunton Park against Carlisle, and another at home against Shrewsbury Town, Wednesday went to Walsall and won 2-0.

Still they suffered from postponements, but by the time they had played 29 matches, they had 29 points and were heading for a mid-table spot. Seven games later, they were still striving to climb into the top half, though they had matches in hand on almost every other club in the division. With half a dozen matches left, however, they were lagging far behind the leaders, and once more the season ended on a note of disappointment. Wednesday had not gone down, but they hadn't exactly pushed for promotion.

Season 1979-80 dawned with a vision of better things, as Wednesday won 3-0 at Barnsley, but then they lost 3-0 at home to Blackburn Rovers. The club with the "yo-yo" reputation was living up to expectations once more. But a 3-1 victory at Plymouth heralded a revival, and at that stage Wednesday and their rivals from Bramall lane, Sheffield United, were going neck and neck to catch the pacesetters.

Once more, though, Wednesday flattered to deceive: they slipped down the table again. Still, hope remained, as they climbed to eighth from the top, although their fans didn't enjoy seeing Sheffield United in pole position. And while Wednesday see-sawed, the Blades continued to lead the promotion race. By the time 16 matches had been played, Wednesday had moved up into fourth place, and if they then slipped a little, at least Sheffield United had been knocked off the top.

Wednesday managed to stay in touch with the leaders as the season headed towards the half-way mark, and by the end of January, reading from the top, it was Grimsby Town, Colchester United, Sheffield United, Chesterfield and Sheffield Wednesday. Then Wednesday edged back into fourth place, with games in hand.

On Saturday, February 23, 1980, Wednesday fans were crowing, having seen their team stick five goals past Rotherham at Hillsborough, while their rivals from Bramall Lane were losing 2-1 at Reading, so Wednesday leap-frogged into third place as they overtook the Blades. And they still had two games in hand on the leaders, Grimsby and Colchester.

On Saturday, March 1, Wednesday won 2-0 at Oxford and climbed above Colchester, and one week later they hit the top as they beat Wimbledon 3-1 at Hillsborough. To add to their satisfaction, Sheffield United had dropped down to sixth place. Then Wednesday and Grimsby contested the leadership in alternate weeks as the season drew towards its close.

By the time there were only three or four games to go, the top of the table read: Grimsby Town (played 44 matches) 59 points; Wednesday (played 43) 55 points; Blackburn Rovers (played 42) 55 points. Sheffield United, nine places down the table and on 44 points, were out of it.

By the time Grimsby and Wednesday each had one game left, with Blackburn having a match in hand, none of the three top clubs could be caught. Grimsby had 60 points, Wednesday and Blackburn 57 apiece, while fourth-placed Chesterfield, even with two games left, could muster only 57 if they won them both, and their goal average was inferior.

As it turned out, Grimsby finished as champions, with 62 points, Blackburn claimed second place with 59 points, Wednesday were third with 58 points, and Chesterfield were the unlucky ones; they had done their gallant best, winning their last two matches to total 57 points. So Wednesday were in the Second Division, and aiming for the First.

Coming towards the close of season 1980-81, Wednesday and Blackburn Rovers - promotion companions 12 months previously - were striving to stage a repeat performance, as were Grimsby Town, although West Ham, Notts. County and Luton Town were leading the way, with Luton the most threatened, since the pack chasing them had almost as many points. West Ham were running away with it, 10 points clear of Notts. County. In the final reckoning, promotion went to the Hammers, Notts. County and Swansea City, who came through to claim third place on goal average.

Sheffield Wednesday had to wait until the end of season 1983-84 before, in company with Chelsea and Newcastle United, they were able to rejoice in promotion to the First Division. Chelsea finished at the top, with 88 points, but they pipped Wednesday for the championship of their division only on goal average, while Newcastle, the club Jack Charlton was to manage next, lagged by eight points, as they came third.

Big Jack, indeed, had already departed from Hillsborough, and it was Howard Wilkinson, appointed Wednesday's manager in June, 1983, who could claim the credit for taking the club back into the First Division. Remarkably, Newcastle's emergence with Wednesday and Chelsea from Division 2 was the signal for Arthur Cox to quit his job at St. James' Park, and for Jack Charlton to move in as his successor.

Cox had signed Kevin Keegan - a master-stroke of opportunism - from Southampton, and Newcastle had risen out of the Second Division largely on the back of Keegan, whose performances not only boosted gates and results, but inspired his teammates. They included Terry McDermott, the emerging Chris Waddle, and Peter Beardsley, who had proved to be another bargain buy when he flew in from Vancouver Whitecaps.

But the euphoria of promotion was soon overtaken by controversy as Cox quit, Keegan hung up his boots, and McDermott made his exit from St. James' Park. Jack Charlton, who as a youngster had stood on the terraces to support the Magpies, was persuaded

persuaded back into big-time football, after having taken time off from the game, and he had his own ideas about the way he wanted Newcastle United to play.

There was talk that his ideas included "playing one-two's with God", and the man who had steered Middlesborough out of the Second Division and Sheffield Wednesday out of the Third was handed the job at St. James' Park with this simple brief: "Keep the club in the First Division." He did exactly that, then he packed it all in and left.

By this time he had become a television personality in his own right, with programmes on the outdoors, holidays and coaching, and his approach to the job at Newcastle was in sharp contrast to the methods of the man he had succeeded.

Arthur Cox ate, drank, and breathed football; he lived for the game. But Jack Charlton showed that he could step back from soccer and take a breather now and then. Under their new manager, Newcastle United made a spectacular return to the First Division: within a week, they were lording it over everyone at the top of the table, after having clocked up three straight wins, 3-2 at Leicester, 2-1 against Jack's old club, Sheffield Wednesday, at St. James' Park, and 3-0 at home against Aston Villa.

Chris Waddle was a marksman at Filbert Street and struck twice against Villa in front of more than 31,000 ecstatic Newcastle supporters, while Peter Beardsley slotted home a spot-kick against Sheffield Wednesday and scored against Villa. However, the next two matches were calculated to dampen the enthusiasm of the Geordie supporters, a 2-0 defeat against Arsenal at Highbury was followed by a thumping 5-0 reverse against Manchester United at Old Trafford.

Then Everton went to St. James' Park and won by the odd goal in five, while the Magpies let slip a four-goal lead in their next match, against Queen's Park Rangers at Loftus Road. It was an astonishing game for the fans to watch, and for the players who participated. For Jack Charlton, it must have been galling, and one which gave him plenty of food for thought.

Having seen his team hit the top, he had embarked upon a fishing trip north of the border, flying back for the encounters with Arsenal and Manchester United. Then came the game at Loftus Road, where Waddle - watched from the stand by England manager Bobby Robson - dazzled as he cracked in a hat-trick to send a message to the international team boss that he was good and ready for the call.

That 4-0 half-time lead was whittled away, though, and while Newcastle scored another goal they allowed Rangers to come back and force a 5-5 draw. That result was the signal for Jack Charlton to dip into the transfer market, and he came up with a couple of signings almost straight away, then bought two big fellows for front-line duty.

Pat Heard, who had played for Everton and Aston Villa, was the first arrival; then came Gary Megson, whose father, Don, had been a full-back with Sheffield Wednesday. So far as the Newcastle supporters were concerned, these two signings were not players to put more of a gloss on the team - they were simply regarded as honest workmen.

They could do a job all right, but the supporters wanted more players with the kind of charisma exhibited by a Keegan, a Beardsley or a Waddle. And two later signings - striker Tony Cunningham and the six-foot-four-inch-tall George Reilly, from Watford, didn't excite the fans in the manner that Malcolm Macdonald ("Supermac") and "Wor Jackie" Milburn, not to mention Albert Stubbins, had once done.

The signings of Cunningham - like Pat Heard, he had played for Sheffield Wednesday, although he arrived as a near-£100,000 buy from Manchester City - and Reilly (who brought Watford £200,000) caused the greatest controversy. Cunningham had helped to take Howard Wilkinson's Wednesday team into the First Division, but he was not destined to make a real impact when he arrived on Tyneside. In the meantime, one of Arthur Cox's big-money signings, full-back John Ryan (who had cost more than £220,000 when he left Oldham Athletic), had departed from Newcastle in the opposite direction, as he moved to Hillsborough.

As for Megson, he had been having an unhappy time at Nottingham Forest, where he had been unable to claim a regular first-team spot, so he had jumped at the chance to resurrect his career by joining Newcastle. All in all, however, the Charlton buys didn't produce a rash of enthusiasm from the supporters, even after they had seen Beardsley hit a hat-trick in a 3-1 victory over derby-game rivals Sunderland on New Year's Day.

Just before then, Aston Villa had got their own back, with a 4-0 win on their own ground, and that triumph over Sunderland, in fact, was sandwiched in between three successive defeats (against Villa, West Brom and Arsenal) and then a 4-0 drubbing by Everton at Goodison Park. Then two draws were followed by another defeat, and it was the last day of February before Newcastle chalked up a victory, as they beat Luton Town with a Kenny Wharton goal. Their record then, over a dozen games, proclaimed that they won twice and lost half a dozen times.

Cunningham's first League goal did not come until March 29, when Newcastle beat Watford 3-1, and, ironically, their other marksmen were Reilly and Megson. But then they lost 4-1 at home to Leicester City and 4-2 against Sheffield Wednesday at Hillsborough, while in their final home game they went down 3-2 against Spurs.

Since he was signed, Cunningham had scored one goal in 13 League outings, Reilly had managed three goals in 14 appearances; Waddle's tally was 13 in 35 matches, Beardsley's 17 in 38. Wharton had chipped in with seven goals, Heard had managed a couple, Megson had scored once, and a precocious kid by the name of Paul Gascoigne had made a couple of appearances, against Queen's Park Rangers and Tottenham Hotspur, each time as a substitute.

Chris Waddle, who had been ever-present during 1984, started to miss out on games during the second half of season 1984-85 and, with his contract due to come to an end, transfer talk became the topic of the day. He was to move on to Tottenham, and before many moons had passed, he was to be followed by the footballer who became known the world over as Gazza.

When Waddle made his exit from St. James' Park, there were some vociferous complaints from fans who claimed the club hadn't really tried to keep this home-grown hero happy, when it came to pay. By then he was a fully-fledged international, and when a tribunal set the fee at £590,000, 'Waddler' shook the dust of St. James' Park from his feet and made his way south to the country's capital city and a new career at White Hart Lane.

His departure came about during the close season - and so did the departure of Newcastle United's manager. The Magpies played Sheffield United in a pre-season friendly match, and some 5,000 people turned up for this inauspicious occasion. It was to turn out an occasion which made headline news, however, because some of those spectators made Jack Charlton the target for their displeasure, as they booed him.

So far as Big Jack was concerned, there could be only one sequel to that: he chucked up the job of managing Newcastle United. As he was to tell me: "I didn't need that kind of hassle." It appeared, then, that for him football, certainly big-time football, might well be a thing of the past, but he was to achieve at least as much fame as an international manager as he had done when he was playing for his country.

The job of managing England, though, was to go to someone else, even though Jack Charlton, it was said, would have welcomed the chance to try to take his country to the finals of the World Cup. That distinction was reserved for the Republic of Ireland.

"I Can't Half Pick 'Em!"

The man who was chairman of the England international committee once told me, with a somewhat wry smile: "I can't half pick 'em!" Peter Swales was referring to his days as chairman of Manchester City, and the men he had chosen at various times as his managers at the club. He admitted: "The biggest mistake I made was to sack Tony Book." In fact, he did remain loyal to Book, who was retained in another capacity.

Swales ended up being reviled by many Manchester City supporters as a bitter battle developed, with former player Francis Lee finally ousting the longest-serving club chairman in English football. Swales also came in for some stick, as the saying goes, after Graham Taylor had failed to take England to the finals of the World Cup in 1994. Swales was one of a small committee which had handed Taylor the job of managing the international team.

According to Peter Swales, the task of making a success of the England job is "the hardest job in football. It destroyed Don Revie, Bobby Robson didn't like it one little bit, and Graham Taylor had to live with it." Jack Charlton, a man who would have liked the chance to show what he could do, was ignored when various candidates came under consideration; it was said that his application for the job didn't even merit the courtesy of a reply from the Football Association. More of that later...

So far, England have had eight full-time team bosses, including the latest incumbent, Terry Venables. In order, they were Walter Winterbottom, Alf Ramsey, Joe Mercer, Don Revie, Ron Greenwood, Bobby Robson, Graham Taylor and Terry Venables. Winterbottom's reign lasted from 1946 to 1962, and under him England played 137 matches, winning 78 of them and drawing 32. Alf Ramsey lasted from 1962 to 1974, which meant that he was in charge for 113 matches, of which England won 68 and drew 28. Ramsey achieved lasting fame, of course, as the first, and, so far, only, team boss to have taken England not only to the final of the World Cup, but actually to have won the coveted trophy.

Joe Mercer? His term was brief enough; he did a caretaker job during 1974, and under him England won three and drew three of the seven games played. Then along came Don Revie, whose tenure of office began in 1974 and ended abruptly in 1977, when he made his sensational departure to the United Arab Emirates, leaving a bewildered, and righteously indignant, Football Association to pick up the pieces. Under Revie, England played 29 matches, winning 14 and drawing eight.

Ron Greenwood came next, and he stayed the course from 1977 to 1982, when he made way for Bobby Robson, whose term of office was to extend from 1982 to 1990. Under the urbane Greenwood, England won 33 of the 55 games played and drew a dozen. Under Robson, England went to the semi-finals of the World Cup in 1990, and of the overall total of 95 matches played, they won 47 and drew 29.

Walter Winterbottom was, in some ways, a man before his time. He was scholarly, personable and generally gave the impression of being mild-mannered. He hailed from the Lancashire mill town of Oldham, and after having been appointed as the Football Association's director of coaching, he also became the first manager of England's international team.

In those days, the England management had been shared round by members of the FA Council on an alternating basis, with the help of a club trainer. Winterbottom's appointment as manager, as well as director of coaching, meant that he would be doing two jobs for the price of one.

Ron Greenwood, himself a deep thinker about the game - and a man who, at club level, produced West Ham teams which played flowing football - was to say that Winterbottom influenced English football even long after he had departed for pastures new.

According to Greenwood, the Winterbottom influence "touched many of the clubs from which England called on players to win the World Cup in 1966." However, there came a day during the reign of Winterbottom when England suffered soccer humiliation at the hands of the no-hopers from the United States. In 1950, when England went to contest the World Cup in Brazil, they met the United States side in a match in Belo Horizonte and were beaten 1-0. The date of this soccer calamity: Thursday, June 29, 1950.

It was rated the most embarrassing result in England's history, until the United States, about to contest the World Cup tournament of 1994, inflicted yet another defeat upon an England team, this one managed by Graham Taylor. Oddly enough, back in 1950, Alf Ramsey - the man who was to lead England to World Cup glory in 1966 - was a member of the side stricken at Belo Horizonte.

That defeat in 1950 did not signal the end for Walter Winterbottom, who was given a vote of confidence to carry on. Then came another day of disaster, this time on Wednesday, November 25, 1953, when, at Wembley of all places, Hungary thrashed the home country 6-3. Once again, Alf Ramsey was a member of the England team. As it turned out, it was to be his final appearance on the international scene as a player.

By 1961 Jimmy Hill, one of today's television pundits, was declaring that Winterbottom was a talented and honourable man who deserved to succeed in any profession, but "unfortunately, he has chosen possibly the most difficult job in England. More criticism had been hurled at this one individual than at any other five men in the football game put together."

English football hadn't then reached a stage where the team boss would find himself being referred to as 'Turnip Head' and being slated mercilessly as he tried to answer the cries of rage which defeat by the United States in a pre-World Cup match had brought about. Nor had it reached a stage where an ex-England footballer was being hailed almost as a saint, as he took the Republic of Ireland to the last 16 of the 1994 tournament.

England did reach the quarter-finals of the 1954 competition, in Switzerland; they failed to win a game when they came up against Brazil, Russia and Austria in the 1958 campaign, in Sweden; and they reached the quarter-finals in Chile, in 1962. Winterbottom subsequently left the Football Association, and Alf Ramsey was appointed as England team manager in his place.

Ramsey's record speaks for itself, although during the later days of his reign he was made to suffer when England came up against Poland in the World Cup: a goalkeeper whom Brian Clough termed "a clown" defied Ramsey's men at Wembley. His name was Jan Tomaszewski, who conceded only one goal, as England hit post and bar and won no fewer than 26 corners. Apart from all this, the 'keeper made saves with fists, feet and other parts of his body, to earn his country a 1-1 draw.

The so-called "clown" did more than that: this result meant that England were no longer contestants in the World Cup, and so

Alf Ramsey (knighted to great acclaim after his 1966 triumph) took the brunt of the criticism. Ramsey lost his job, and the recently-appointed secretary of the Football Association, Ted Croker, received a phone call from Leeds manager Don Revie to say that he would like to talk about his chances of succeeding Ramsey.

During the interim period, genial "Uncle Joe" Mercer took charge of the England team, and while three other managers, Gordon Milne, Gordon Jago and Jimmy Bloomfield, were considered as the next incumbents of the job, once Revie had indicated his interest, the search was effectively over. Like Ramsey's achievements in 1966, Revie's success at club level told its own story.

Alan Hardaker, whom I knew well as secretary of the Football League, could be irascible and dogmatic, and he certainly didn't approve of the appointment of Revie, with whom he had tangled on previous occasions. Revie also came in for criticism from the players he chose for England, not least for the dossiers he presented to them about the opposition. In 29 games he used 52 players, only once fielding an unchanged team.

During his time with England, Revie and the chairman of the Football Association, Professor Sir Harold Thompson, said some harsh things about each other, and there was the famous tale of their meeting, early on in Revie's England career, when Sir Harold told him that "when I get to know you better, Revie, I shall call you Don." To which Revie retorted: "When I get to know you better, Thompson, I shall call you Sir Harold."

As time went by, there was little love lost, and when Revie began to suspect that his days as the England boss were numbered, he took swift action, landing a job with the United Arab Emirates at a reputed salary of £340,000 and a four-year contract, and leaving the Football Association to learn from a front-page story in the Daily Mail that he had defected.

Revie's explanation: "I sat down with my wife one night, and we agreed the job was no longer worth all the aggravation. It was bringing too much heartache to those nearest to us. Nearly everyone in the country seemed to want me out. So I am giving them what they want. I know people will accuse me of running away, but the situation has become impossible."

Not only was Revie accused of having run away; he was accused of being mercenary, and newspapers attempted to revive accusations that during his time with Leeds United he had offered improper financial inducements to enable his own team to win matches.

I have no knowledge of this, although I worked for one of the papers concerned, The People. I do know that when Don Revie was offered cash to supply information to a national newspaper, he politely but firmly declined. That was certainly to his credit, all the more so since it has long been an established fact that newspapers are ever-ready to pay people in football for information, whether it be an exclusive transfer-request story or something more unsavoury.

My paper once dug into a Cup final ticket "scandal", and I was told that one of my closest contacts was involved. I phoned him to let him know that he could expect a visit from one of our news reporters, though I didn't reveal why. Later, my contact told me: "You'll still always be welcome in my home, but don't ever come on business from your paper."

People with whom Don Revie had had close contact while he was with Leeds had something to say about his defection to the Middle East. One man defended him by saying Revie had wanted to make sure his family was looked after and that he wasn't being greedy; another man, a former player, reckoned that Revie hadn't done himself justice by bowing out the way he did. I never saw anything from Jack Charlton, but it would have been interesting to hear what he thought about the doings of the man who, in so many ways, had been his mentor at Leeds.

After Revie, it was Ron Greenwood, and then came Bobby Robson, and it was during the latter's time as England manager that his team came up against Jack Charlton's Republic of Ireland side in World Cup competition. This was in Italy, in 1990, when the two countries clashed in the first round. The venue for the match was Cagliari.

England had not conceded one goal in qualifying games against Sweden, Poland and Albania, and they met six countries, Italy, Yugoslavia, Brazil, Czechoslovakia, Denmark and Uruguay, in warm-up matches, winning four of these and drawing one. The defeat came against Uruguay. The first-round opener against the Republic of Ireland in Cagliari was reckoned to be one which Robson's men should and would win.

After that match - a Gary Lineker goal ensured a 1-1 draw - one tabloid newspaper in England demanded: "Bring them home!"

Robson and his men had to counter a hostile media, as well as the opposition on the football field, and Jack Charlton's team did England no favours by extracting a point from them. England's side contained such illustrious names as Beardsley, Barnes, Lineker, Robson (Bryan) and Gascoigne, the cheeky chappie Charlton had left behind when he quit Newcastle United.

Lineker's goal came after play had been going for only eight minutes, and some people expected England to follow up with a hatful. Instead, it was Peter Shilton who was beaten, 15 minutes from full time, as Everton's Kevin Sheedy, a midfield man with a deadly left foot, notched an equaliser. The following day, the English papers delivered their verdict, and it wasn't at all complimentary.

Next, England tackled Holland, and the result was a scoreless draw. Holland had also drawn (1-1) with Egypt, and 24 hours after the England-Holland encounter it was the turn of the Irish to see what they could do against Egypt. In Palermo, there were no goals, and this meant that the first four matches in the group had all been drawn, with the four teams each having an identical record.

So England needed to beat Egypt, and the Republic were looking for a victory against the Dutch. It was Mark Wright, scoring his first international goal, who clinched victory for Bobby Robson's team, with a climbing header from an accurately taken free-kick by Paul Gascoigne, while in the other game the Republic and Holland drew 1-1. While England topped the group, the luck of the draw left the Republic of Ireland in second place.

From then on, it was sudden death all the way, and England managed to survive some alarms and excursions before finally bowing out at the semi-final stage, beaten 4-3 by West Germany in a penalty shoot-out. Jack Charlton's team got as far as the quarter-finals, after having won a penalty shoot-out against Romania, thanks to a spot-kick goal from David O'Leary.

The killer blow for the Republic came when they played in the Eternal City of Rome, where they came up against the host nation backed by the vociferous support of thousands of partisan Italians. At that stage of the tournament, Jack Charlton and his players could feel proud of what they had achieved, and they were not to be disgraced against the Italians.

In this, their first stab at the World Cup finals, the Republic had reached the last eight by way of three draws and a penalty

shoot-out, but the road to Rome concluded their World Cup journey, as a Sicilian by the name of "Toto" Schillaci, who played for
Juventus, scored the goal which won the match. Jack Charlton and
his merry men, who had been given tremendous support by an army
of Irish fans, returned home amid clouds of glory. Bobby Robson
bowed out of World Cup management when he resumed his role as
a club boss, this time with PSV Eindhoven, in Holland.

Peter Swales, chairman of the England international committee, told me that while the England job "destroyed" Don Revie,
Bobby Robson "didn't like it one little bit", either. In this, I feel
that Swales was probably overstating the case, because Robson
himself, who had confirmed in advance that he would be leaving
his post after the 1990 World Cup, explained: "I'm going because
I didn't think there would be a job here." It appeared that FA chairman Sir Bert Millichip had not felt able to give Robson the assur-
ances he would have liked about staying in the England post.

And so England had to consider whom they might appoint as
the next occupant of the hot seat. Naturally, the media was happy
to supply plenty of names as possibles, but when all came to all,
and the list of candidates was whittled down, three names were left:
Graham Taylor, the manager of Aston Villa; Howard Kendall, the
manager of Manchester City; and Joe Royle, the manager of
Oldham Athletic. In the case of Howard Kendall, of course, Peter
Swales was not only the chairman of the England international
committee, but the chairman of Kendall's club, Manchester City.

Kendall had returned to England after having managed
Athletic Bilbao, and Swales had regarded it as a coup to land him
for City. Howard had won the League, the FA Cup and the
European Cup-winners Cup when he was team boss at Everton, and
when he arrived at Maine Road on his return from Spain, Swales
told me: "I've got the best man for the job now."

He truly believed that, and the proof of the pudding was in the
eating, as Howard began to pull the club round towards safety and
respectability, despite some criticism from fans that he was bringing in too many ex-Everton players. When Kendall decided to
return to Goodison Park, he claimed that if City had been a love
affair, Everton was a marriage. Swales was upset at Howard's
decision, but recognised it was no use keeping someone who would
be unhappy to stay.

Back to the England job, however, and the selection committee sat down to ponder upon the three names. The committee consisted of FA chairman Sir Bert Millichip, Dick Wragg (Swales's predecessor as international committee chairman), Swales himself, League president Bill Fox, Arthur McMullen and FA secretary Graham Kelly.

It didn't take long to discover that so far as Millichip was concerned, his vote would go to Graham Taylor, whose credentials were impressive: he had taken Watford up to the First Division (they then went to the FA Cup final and were runners-up in the title chase). And when Millichip departed for a meeting of UEFA, Swales, Fox, McMullen and Kelly did the next part of the job: they got Graham Taylor in for an interview.

By that time, Howard Kendall had given indications that, after all, he was committing himself to management at club level, while Joe Royle, who had worked wonders on a shoestring at Oldham, was listed as someone who, at a future date, might well finish as the leading name for the job. But right now, the men interviewing Graham Taylor came to the same conclusion as Millichip had done.

He WAS the man for the job, even though, as it turned out, the Football Association would be required to pay Aston Villa no less than £225,000 as compensation for losing a team boss whose contract still had a year to run. Indeed, Villa chairman Doug Ellis had been seeking at least twice as much as the Football Association had in mind.

Finally, Graham Taylor was installed as the successor to Bobby Robson. He was given a four-year contract and, at the age of 45, committed himself to the task ahead. Instead of striving to steer Aston Villa to success in the UEFA Cup, he would be doing his level best to get results with England in both the 1992 European championships and, more importantly, in the World Cup finals of 1994.

For the first time in its history, the Football Association had been called upon to pay what might be regarded as a "transfer fee" in order to land a manager, and Peter Swales and company fervently hoped that they had made the right decision.

Swales, indeed, told me even while Graham Taylor was struggling to see England through to the World Cup finals in the United States, that he still believed the former Villa boss was "the right man for the job." The critics were not to be so tolerant, as results went from bad to worse. In fact, the jibes were to be cutting, with

Swales and Taylor being bracketed as the villains of the piece. Yes, hard words were spoken and written.

What made it all the harder to swallow, of course, was that while England floundered unhappily, as Graham Taylor sought to achieve his goal, the Republic of Ireland moved steadily forward towards the World Cup finals of '94. England had been dumped out of the European championships by Sweden in 1992, and the day came when they had to meet Holland in a bid to save their World Cup skins in 1994.

To be fair, the Dutch got away with it on that occasion, as Ronald Koeman escaped a red card and then added insult to injury by scoring from a twice-taken free-kick. Talk about kicking a team when it's down!

There was a school of thought, even before it was realised that England were not only down, but out of the World Cup, that Graham Taylor should be sacked and someone else brought in to finish the job while there was still time to qualify. But Peter Swales rejected that approach as he gave Taylor a vote of confidence, reasoning that there remained three matches to be won, and that "we know he is not a quitter."

Quitter or not, Graham Taylor had the mortification of seeing Jack Charlton's Irish rise to the occasion as they won six and drew three of their World Cup qualifying group games. Indeed, around the end of season 1992-93, they went to Albania, Latvia and Lithuania, and won each time out. Now those three nations may not be the strongest in the world when it comes to playing football, but they all have to be fought and vanquished, and, as was pointed out at the time, Jack Charlton was in exactly the same situation as Graham Taylor, in that the players at his disposal all had to come from the same background, a background where you played games right through the season until you were almost leg-weary with football.

It was also said, with perfect truth, that Jack Charlton, whose choice was more limited than his opposite number in the England camp, devised a system from which he could get the best out of the men at his disposal. He laid down the tactics, and the players all knew their roles.

Some of his Irishmen had other accents (Scottish and Merseyside, for instance), but they knew what was required of them when it came to ensuring that the Republic qualified for the

World Cup. And if Paul McGrath was a "Problem boy", on occasion, Big Jack was still prepared to accommodate him when there was a pressing need for a player of his talent.

Liam Brady, a gifted footballer in his day and a knowledgeable manager since he hung up his boots, was one who had discovered that Jack Charlton could also be ruthless. Brady was pulled off in his final international match (his benefit game, and a friendly) even before the half-time whistle had gone, and he was to observe that "you play Jack Charlton's way, or you don't play at all."

By 1993, the Republic of Ireland were being given a ranking of sixth in the world, while England could do no better than merit eleventh place in the FIFA listings, and that support the Irish fans gave to Charlton and his men on the way to and during the 1994 World Cup was in stark contrast to the manner in which Graham Taylor and his England players were to suffer the slings and arrows of their supporters' displeasure.

Anyone who watched the television film of Graham Taylor's trek away from the World Cup and into oblivion, in so far as the England job was concerned, could scarcely help but feel sorry for the man, especially when he was seen to suggest that his job was at the mercy of a refereeing decision which had gone against England.

Anyone who watched as the Republic gifted two goals to Holland in the World Cup quarter-finals must have felt for Jack Charlton, as he was seen to half-turn away while mouthing his disgust at the way things had gone for his adopted country. Yet, at least, he and his men had been to the finals. Not so Graham Taylor and England.

Which, of course, poses the all-important, all-embracing question: WHY did Jack Charlton, a World Cup winner with England in 1966, never appear to come under consideration for the job of managing England? Especially when he seemed to want to do the job.

He had managed Middlesbrough, Sheffield Wednesday and Newcastle United, so the experience at club level was there. He had taken Wednesday out of the Third Division, Middlesbrough out of the Second, and, in a game where, even by 1970, managerial jobs had changed hands 700 times, he had never been sacked. He had played in 35 international matches, too, so at all levels of the game he knew what was wanted. Why, then, did he miss out on the England job?

Now We'll Never Know

With Jack Charlton, what you see is what you get. Or is it? Does the outward directness mask a certain amount of deviousness in his make-up, for instance? Let me say here and now that in all my dealings with him, I never found him to be other than straight-forward, calling the shots as he saw them. And certainly he has made no bones about his attitude and his decisions, when he has felt the occasion has called for straight talking.

At the same time, it was fair to question why he talked about sitting down and thinking about things, when he was due to return home from the 1994 World Cup. He said he wanted to get the feel of things, to see if the Irish really wanted him to stay on and steer them towards the European championships in 1996.

Jack must surely have known, without having to ask anybody, that the Irish fans hung on to just about every word he spoke, and I wasn't in the least surprised to read a back-page story which said that "Ireland pleaded with Jack Charlton to stay on as manager today, despite seeing their team crash out of the World Cup last night."

It was said that Big Jack would assess the mood of the Irish on his arrival back in Dublin, after a week-end report that he was ready to quit as manager. It was also said that the feeling was that he would love to have a crack at the next big international event, the European championships in England. Jack's reaction: "I have no intention of leaving the job at the moment, but I have to get back to Ireland and find out what the feeling is there."

When Jack and 19 of his 22-man squad of players did arrive back, it was to find a reception committee headed by the Irish Prime Minister, Albert Reynolds, and a host of fans - estimated at more than 100,000 - when manager and players took their bow at Phoenix Park, Dublin.

Their mood was clear enough - "We want Big Jack to stay!" And Big Jack almost obliged when he said that he'd spend a month or so sitting down and weighing up matters, although he felt that he would like to remain as the Republic of Ireland manager. He was a grand-dad, he was coming up to 60, but maybe one more crack, this time at the European championships, was what he would fancy.

It was suggested around that time that what Big Jack would also fancy was a chance to tweak the noses of the English hosts, to pull the tail of the bulldog, as he pitted his brains and his team against the tactics and the players employed by Terry Venables, who had a few things to say on that score, himself.

Even before the 1994 World Cup had come to its conclusion, Jack Charlton and Terry Venables were on opposite sides, as they embarked upon a series of television appearances. Venables was working for the BBC, Big Jack (after his team's exit at the last-16 stage of the tournament) returned from Ireland to resume his role as a television pundit for ITV.

Venables said: "I'm told Jack wants to tweak the noses of the English in the European championship. I'm looking forward to pitting my wits against him." Of course, Venables could afford to smile, because he was team boss of the host nation, which didn't need to qualify, while the Republic still had to surmount several hurdles in order to get to the finals.

Terry did say also: "Jack has done a great job, and I sincerely hope he wins qualification for the finals in 1996, but I have to think about tweaking the noses of all the finalists; as hosts, England have to do well." No-one knew this better than he did, after the fiasco of failure to qualify for the 1994 World Cup.

Venables paid Jack Charlton this tribute, too: "Qualification (for the 1994 World Cup) from a tough group provided a continuation of the respectability established during his eight years as manager. They provided optimism and enjoyment for so many people, although the professional would have been disappointed, because they wanted to win again (against Holland)."

It was reported then that, privately, Jack Charlton was "fuming" at the way in which his team had gone out of the tournament: two goals gifted to the Dutch. It was also said that while almost certainly announcing his retirement before the next World Cup, Charlton's desire to bow out of the international arena on English soil, at the conclusion of the 1996 European championships, would prove "too powerful to resist."

By that time he would be 61, and he would have completed 10 years as the Republic team boss. During that time he had estab-

lished the Irish as a force in world football. It was said, and right-
ly so, that "an incredible bond has been forged between Charlton
and the people of Ireland. His ambition was not to disappoint them
in America, and the warmth of the acclaim he received in the
Orlando Citrus Bowl after the defeat by Holland dispelled any such
fear. How dearly they would love to see him humble the English at
Wembley."

However, it was also pointed out that after USA '94, "the
sobering reality is that Irish supporters now expect so much that
there is serious pressure on the team and the manager to keep performing miracles", and that changes would have to be made. For
one thing, heads were likely to roll after the blunders against the
Dutch; for another, age was catching up with several of the players
in the Irish team, "players such as Pat Bonner, Paul McGrath, Ray
Houghton and John Sheridan have reached the end of the international road."

By the same token, the World Cup of '94 had thrown up new
and younger names. "Charlton should have his eye on the future,
which now rests in the hands of youngsters like Bolton's Jason
McAteer, Gary Kelly, of Leeds United, and Coventry City's Phil
Babb, who all made outstanding contributions." That they did.

There was no doubting the mood of the Football Association
of Ireland, too. "We'd like to have Jack as manager for as long as
he wants to stay," declared chief executive Sean Connolly. Then,
perhaps significantly, he added: "Jack has NEVER had a contract,
it has always been a gentleman's agreement. If he wanted to give
up, we wouldn't try to stand in his way. But we'd love to think of
Jack as a long-term appointment."

Which brings us to the question of why he never got the
chance to manage England.

Jack Charlton has been described as "a loose cannon," and it
has been suggested that the Football Association was so shattered
by the defection of Don Revie that there was no way it would ever
allow a situation such as that to happen again. The managers who
followed, it was claimed, were all men whose loyalty to the cause
was absolute.

No-one would ever suggest, of course, that Jack Charlton's
loyalty to the cause was anything other than absolute. He had
demonstrated that loyalty with hundreds of games as a one-club
man, by his appearance on 35 occasions for England, by sticking

with the Republic of Ireland for eight years. He had also demonstrated that he would have liked the England job; after all, he did apply for it, after Don Revie had thrown in the sponge.

It's fair to ask if the Football Association felt that the Leeds United connection, Don Revie and Jack Charlton, was not conducive to naming Big Jack as the manager of England. It's fair, also, to ask if the Football Association felt that he wouldn't want to be tied down to a contract and, in that case, if he would suddenly decide to "do a Revie", not because he wished to defect to foreign climes for a better job, but because the mood had taken him to quit.

After all, he had turned his back on Newcastle United when the fans there had started to get on his back. If the England supporters decided to get on Big Jack's back, would he then shrug his shoulders and tell them he "didn't need that kind of hassle?" And would the fans want Jack Charlton as England's team manager, if they found that his players were not turning on some sort of style but, rather, were performing simply as a unit designed to get results?

These are all legitimate questions to ask, and there are a couple of other points to consider, too. There's an old saying that "it could only happen in Ireland", and Jack Charlton's success there may have been one of those things that "could only have happened" in the country across the Irish Sea. An Englishman taking charge and rubbing the noses of the English in the mire. What's more, he chose another Englishman, Maurice Setters, as his second in command.

There is another old saying, this one culled from the Bible, that "many are called, few are chosen." In Jack Charlton's case, he wasn't called to Lancaster Gate after having sought the job of England team manager, but he was most certainly chosen to lead the Irish to glory.

If the mantle of club manager never seemed to fit Jack Charlton too comfortably, the same could probably be said about brother Bobby, who didn't stay too long in the job after he had been appointed team boss at Preston North End. Like Jack, Bobby has seemed happiest on the world stage - in his case, as a roving ambassador for football, as well as in his role as a director of a world-famous club, Manchester United.

Normally mild-mannered and reticent, he didn't mince words after Sweden had despatched England from the European championships in 1992 - Gary Lineker was pulled off at a time when he was on 48 goals and bidding to draw level with Bobby Charlton's record of 49. After England's inglorious exit, Bobby posed the question: "Whatever happened to football? You know, passing, that sort of thing."

When England were due to tackle Norway - with elimination from the 1994 World Cup a very real threat - the danger signals were indeed flashing, and after disaster had struck Graham Taylor's team yet again, Bobby Charlton was saying: "We were technically naive, unprofessional in everything we did. It was a performance that really plumbed the depths. What really hurts a lot of people is not that they lost the match, but the way they lost it. We always seem to pride ourselves on being aggressive, tough, professional and brave. Those were all the qualities we were lacking."

Arguments were put forward then that Graham Taylor should go, but Peter Swales, chairman of the international committee, remained loyal to his man as he said: "The World Cup campaign isn't over yet, we have three matches left, and it's still feasible that we might qualify."

At an even later stage Graham Kelly, the Football Association's chief executive, was counselling people to "sit tight" and wait and see what happened. What happened in the final analysis was that Holland defeated England 2-0 in Rotterdam and that the Dutch went to Poland and beat the opposition in Poznan to clinch qualification for the World Cup finals. Even a last-fling 7-1 victory by England over San Marino failed to salvage a place in the finals.

For the Football Association, as well as for the supporters and the players of England, that failure to qualify was a grievous blow, not least because of the loss of income entailed. Quietly, people Stateside might have been sighing with relief in the knowledge that there was much less chance of hooligans from England wreaking damage during the World Cup, but England's failure was still a savage blow to the folks back home.

Of course, something had to be done, and the sequel to the whole sorry story of England's attempts to qualify came on November 23, 1993. That will surely be a date engraved on Graham Taylor's heart, for it was the day he, and his assistant, Lawrie McMenemy, handed in their resignations. There was also another departure: that of Peter Swales as chairman of the international committee.

He had stuck with Taylor to the bitter end, and for Swales, the end was bitter, indeed; he was ousted from his job as chairman of Manchester City, as well, and suffered not only abuse, but threats suggesting that his life was in danger. Today, he can look back upon it all as an enlightening and chastening experience.

I have known him for 30 years or more, since the days when he and Noel White (a director of Liverpool and Swales's successor as chairman of the international committee), were partners in business, after they had pooled their demob money. Swales, the son of a fishmonger, lived over the shop; later, he came to have a fine house in the leafy suburbs of Cheshire.

With Noel White, he went into the sheet-music and record business, stayed on when one of the giants of industry bought them out (White took over an hotel), and eventually decided that he preferred being a big fish in a little pool again, so he went back into business on his own. He is virtually a workaholic - as a rule, he takes a week's holiday at the same hotel in Jersey each year - and while on the footballing side he has surely made mistakes, so far as I could judge, during the many years he was chairman of Manchester City, he always tried to do his best for the club. Not least because he was a fan.

At the height of the Maine Road troubles, he said: "I don't mind the booing, I can take that, and I expect criticism. But I don't like people throwing things (he had just been pelted with eggs). Even so, I feel deeply for the fans. I understand their feelings."

Swales was villified for having sacked so many managers during his time at Manchester City, and he confessed to me that his biggest mistake was in firing Tony Book - "I should have given him time to turn things round." After the axe had fallen upon Peter Reid, one of Swales's fiercest critics was Johnny Giles, the former Manchester United and Leeds United star who achieved managerial success as well as international acclaim when he played for the Republic of Ireland.

Swales was so stung by Giles's criticisms that he replied publicly to them. Giles had said: "Swales appoints managers and then denies them the power to manage." His track record was "one, long example of how to get it wrong." In reply, Swales claimed he had always given his managers 100 per cent support: "In fact, I have probably given them too much freedom in the past, when you analyse the spending I have authorised." Swales then listed the cash outlay during Howard Kendall's stewardship (close on £4.5M), and what had been spent while Peter Reid was the team manager (around £7.5M).

He averred that he had supported Malcolm Allison, John Bond, Billy McNeill and Mel Machin, too, and reminded Giles of the big-money signings such as Steve Daley (£1.75M), Kevin Reeves (£1.1M), and Trevor Francis (£1.2M), claiming that Manchester City were the first club to have signed three players valued at £1M. "City were recognised as the biggest spenders in football, attracting the best internationals."

Swales declared: "No other chairman in the Premiership has allowed his managers the freedom over the past 19 years that I have given." Swales referred to Giles as "a failed manager", and in answer to that charge the little Irishman said: "I am happy for my career as a player, coach and manager to be judged by football men of more weight than you. I stand by every line of my criticism of you."

So much for trading punches at club level. When it came to the international arena, Swales came in for more biting criticism as the man who, it was claimed, had said on one occasion that England would qualify "easily" for the 1994 World Cup finals and who, it was also claimed, had indicated that it might have been what could be termed a blessing in disguise that England had not gone further than the semi-finals, in Italy in 1990.

According to Peter Swales, Robson couldn't take the pressure. The way Swales put it to me was that when it came to the England job, Bobby Robson "didn't like it one little bit." Personally, while I have always got on well with Peter Swales, I have also always had a soft spot for Bobby Robson, who treated me with the utmost courtesy on the first occasion I ever spoke to him, and he could have been forgiven then for giving me a polite, but firm brush-off.

Ipswich Town, then under Robson's management, were due to play Manchester United at Old Trafford on the Saturday afternoon, and on the evening before the game the Daily Mail rang me and asked if I would go down to the Ipswich team's hotel and interview a young player there. His name was George Burley, he was just 17, and he was scheduled to make his debut the following afternoon against, of all people, George Best.

I didn't know Bobby Robson, but I phoned the hotel, got him

out of the restaurant, and put it to him. Could I come down and talk to young George Burley? Now, Robson could easily have told me that the lad was under enough pressure, since he was about to face up to Best, but he agreed straight away to let me speak to Burley, and I went down and did the interview. He was rooming with Kevin Beattie, another of Ipswich Town's home-produced starlets at that time, and I got my story. So I was grateful to Bobby Robson for being so co-operative.

When it came down to picking a successor to him as the England manager, three names were in the frame: Howard Kendall, Joe Royle and Graham Taylor. I am given to understand that Howard, whom I have known for years, finally decided not to push his claims, and when I talked to Joe Royle about his hat being in the ring he told me: "I was invited to be interviewed, and I felt flattered that my name had come up for consideration, but in the end I didn't think it was worth going in for the job, at that time. I didn't feel I was ready for it; I was a Second Division manager, but we hadn't won anything, and, in any case, I wasn't ready to give up the day-to-day involvement that you get when you're a club manager. So I wrote to decline the opportunity, while indicating that if it came up again at some future stage, the situation might well be different, from my point of view."

So Graham Taylor got the job and, as Peter Swales said, he "had to live with it." Bobby Charlton, who had voiced his criticisms after England's poor showing in the 1992 European championships, had something to say, also, when the England manager was being urged from all sides to pick Chris Waddle for the crucial World Cup qualifier against Holland at Wembley. At that time, Waddle had played a starring role for Sheffield Wednesday as they went to Wembley three times for two Cup finals.

When England met Holland in April, 1993, Waddle's name wasn't on the team sheet, however, and Bobby Charlton expressed his "sheer disbelief" that Taylor had overlooked the Wednesday winger: "I can't understand why he isn't being given the chance. I imagine the Dutch will be pleased; Waddle has the type of skills which aren't widespread in our game."

Charlton was joined in his condemnation of Taylor's act of omission when Gary Lineker argued: "I've been saying since I retired that Waddle would be in any side of mine, and so would Peter Beardsley. I don't think age matters if they're the best players, and for me, both still are."

Lineker, himself discarded by Graham Taylor after an exceptional run of scoring successes in an England shirt, claimed: "I don't believe it's a football issue. I just don't think they really get on. It's as simple as that. I think it's more of a personality clash; Chris is quite opinionated in the game, and there's nothing wrong with that. There's no reason, football-wise, why he shouldn't be in the squad, it's inconceivable, especially with the form he's been displaying for a few seasons now, but particularly this season. He's been outstanding for Sheffield Wednesday. I can understand the manager's argument that he doesn't want to change a winning team. The one thing we need is a steady side, but he would be a nice player to have on the bench."

Well, Waddle dazzled in Wednesday's FA Cup semi-final against Sheffield United, and England let a two-goal lead slip away against Holland, but Waddle failed to inspire Wednesday to victory in their three Cup tussles with Arsenal. Then again, England gave a mediocre performance against Poland in Katowice, and emerged from their World Cup defeat against Norway being badly mauled by the media.

So, dependent upon your point of view, it could be argued that "Waddler" flattered to deceive, or that England should have kept him under wraps, ready to release him against the Dutch. For me, too often in the finals against Arsenal Chris Waddle was caught going nowhere, and too seldom did we see the imaginative approach, with Waddle beating his man by sheer skill - yet there isn't a shadow of doubt that Chris possesses this quality in abundance.

It's interesting to see that David Pleat claimed some credit for having turned Waddle into the player who cost Marseille £4M. After having had a disappointing season playing wide on the left for Spurs, Waddle was switched to the opposite flank. Pleat recalled: "He seemed to have a mental block about playing on the left: when he got the ball, he'd stop and wiggle, then decide what to do. But when he swapped sides he would take it in his stride and run with it. He was so much more comfortable playing right, or in a free role."

One wonders what Jack Charlton would have done, had he been England's team boss, or had he been able to make use of Waddle's services for the Republic of Ireland. We shall never know. Neither shall we know just what kind of a job Big Jack would have done as the manager of England, although Peter Swales admits: "I suppose he should have been given an interview."

Swales's recollection is that Jack Charlton was in the frame at the same time as Brian Clough, when Ron Greenwood was finishing and Bobby Robson got the job. Swales says: "I don't know why Jack Charlton didn't get an interview, although I feel sure that he would have been sent a reply to any application." Somewhat wryly, Swales also says: "There are a lot of things you can put right, with hindsight."

Although he was ousted from the top job at Manchester City and handed over the chairmanship of the England international committee to Noel White, Swales remains a man on the inside of football at the highest level: he is a vice-president of the Football Association and, as such, he is a member of the FA Council and of the international committee.

Swales agrees that Howard Kendall pulled out before matters had reached the interview stage and that it was "cut and dried" for Graham Taylor to take over from Bobby Robson.

"The managers we have had while I have been involved with England were what I'd call knocking bets to get the job - even Don Revie. They all looked good bets when they got the job, and I stuck with Graham Taylor because I thought he could do the job. I think he would have done it, with a bit of luck, too. I don't feel he got the breaks, and the whole thing just turned against him. He was trying to do something with probably not the best players we had ever had, and it didn't work out."

Swales maintains that he was misunderstood when he was said to have offered the view that it was a good thing England didn't reach the final in 1990, because that would have meant four more years of Bobby Robson. "I didn't actually say that; I said I felt that we needed a fresh face in the job, so from that point of view it was probably a good job he didn't succeed in taking England all the way. I wasn't knocking Bobby Robson as much as saying we needed a fresh face. His record now says he was better than Graham Taylor, but that is with hindsight. I thought Graham Taylor had the better potential, but it didn't work out that way. And for my money, we had a bit of luck in 1990."

Should Terry Venables step down tomorrow, for whatever reason, would Jack Charlton's name come into the frame? "No, he's coming up to 60, and I don't think he'd say 'Yes', any way. At the time he was being talked about as an England manager, he wasn't one of the obvious choices - Bobby Robson was considered to be far better. I think Jack Charlton has done remarkably well, but he was probably made for that particular job (with the Republic of Ireland). Bill Shankly was born to manage Liverpool, Don Revie to manage Leeds, he certainly wasn't born to be the England manager, and I believe Jack Charlton was born to be the Republic of Ireland manager. I wouldn't say I know him as well as a lot of people, but I have come across him from time to time, and he's never shown any sign of animosity towards me. One thing about him which did strike me: he always appears to be extremely confident."

Peter Swales himself has never been short on confidence, nor has he shunned publicity, for the most part. Swales and Charlton working together in the highest echelons of English football? It would have been a fascinating sight, to say the least, because both are strong-willed men and, had there been fundamental disagreements, surely something would have had to give. However, we shall never know how England would have fared under Big Jack. What we do know is what was accomplished by the team that Jack built, across the Irish Sea.

"Stop Complaining"

Different people see Jack Charlton in different ways. He's made people laugh; he's made people angry; he's made people almost cry. One of his endearing traits at times has been the way he's apparently forgotten the name of someone who is virtually a household word, or got the name wrong. He was once heard to refer to Paul McGrath as John McGrath, for instance. Paul, of course was a key player in Big Jack's 1994 World Cup team; John was once a centre-half, as well. He played for Newcastle United, then managed clubs such as Bury, Preston North End and Halifax Town.

I remember John McGrath - like Jack Charlton, a witty after-dinner speaker - for a good reason. The first time I ever met him as a manager, I collared him after the game and asked if he could spare a minute for "a quick word or two." "Sure," he replied - then said: ".... off!" And asked : "How's that?" Since the whole episode was accompanied by a broad grin, I couldn't take offence, and John McGrath then proceeded to give me a proper interview.

Jack Charlton had a pithy retort, too, for one of the players he had at Middlesbrough - David Mills. There was a newspaper report that Liverpool were ready to shell out £200,000 for Mills (who later joined West Brom for £500,000), so he went to ask Big Jack about it. Middlesborough's manager admitted that Liverpool had offered £200,000, but he said it wasn't enough - he'd turned it down.

Now, Mills hadn't cost Boro' a penny, and he reckoned that if he couldn't join Liverpool he was at least worth more money if he stayed at Ayresome Park. According to Mills, Jack Charlton uttered a two-word expletive and walked out of the office, leaving the player still sitting there.

It was David Mills who confirmed my suspicion that Big Jack had a habit of cadging cigarettes from people like me. Mills once recalled an occasion when Boro' had travelled to London for a game and they were having a training session in Hyde Park. Mills said that Jack approached a total stranger who was sitting on a bench and asked if he could "borrow a fag." He got one, too.

There was another story, this time about Jack's penchant for going shooting. According to David Mills, Big Jack at times would find the Boro' apprentices a job of work to do, other than football: he'd get them to act as "beaters" when he went game-shooting on the moors. Mills recalled that even though he was a senior professional, he got roped in for this task one winter's day, when he was on the injury list.

Mills didn't get his rise after Jack had rejected that £200,000 offer for him from Liverpool, but he maintained that he still got on well with Boro's manager, he even followed him to Sheffield Wednesday and lodged with the Charltons until he found accommodation of his own. While there, he was given the chore of feeding the hens, and found himself penned in by the sheep. He made his escape by chucking hen feed at the sheep in order to distract them.

Mills echoed the comments of Liam Brady when he said: "Jack would stand by you, if you did what he wanted, even if you failed. I was never dropped by him at Boro' or at Wednesday." And referring to Jack Charlton's ascent to be manager at international level, Mills pointed out that he "never has to discuss a contract, never to sign a player. It's perfect. He just has to get them to play."

Former League referee Peter Rhodes was like Jack Charlton: a tough nut, in his day. Malcolm Allison was banned from the touchline, after Rhodes had reported him; Billy Bingham (later to manage Northern Ireland and pit his wits against Big Jack at World Cup level) got the red card from Rhodes, so did Denis Law and Ian St. John.

Rhodes recalls: "Billy Bingham was playing in a game against Bangu, the Brazilian champions, when I was refereeing in the States. An opponent fouled him after Billy had beaten him all ends up. Billy retaliated by planting a perfect uppercut into the opponent's solar-plexus. Billy had to go."

Rhodes braved the wrath of the Anfield faithful, to give St. John his marching orders for retaliation, and when Manchester United were in action, Law was told to walk. Rhodes recalls: "Law fouled Ball, and I gave a free-kick. I walked alongside Denis and when I spoke to him, I received a rude answer. Paddy Crerand came up to Denis and said: "You don't swear at this referee.""

whereupon Denis replied, "Why not? - He's a real....!"

That was the signal for Rhodes to dispense with the services of Denis Law for the remainder of the match, and the United star was fined and banned. Ask Rhodes what he thought about the refereeing in the 1994 World Cup and he says it's like comparing an ordinary driver with a racing driver: different skills are needed at a modest 50 miles an hour to those required at 170 miles an hour.

"It's as if many of those referees had been driving family saloons around their own neck of the woods, then the standard has suddenly been upped, as they are asked to perform on the world stage. You can't blame the referees, really, they shouldn't be picked one from each country. If you've got five from the same country who are outstanding, then pick them all."

Ask Rhodes about Jack Charlton and the World Cup, and he says: "I think he was a pain in the ass. He couldn't complain about being fined. He got his comeuppance. He was the only one who didn't turn up for the FIFA session which laid down all the rules and regulations for the tournament. And when you look back at what the Republic of Ireland achieved, everything hinged on that one speculative kick by Ray Houghton which brought the winner against Italy."

"If that hadn't gone in, the Irish would have been catching the plane home. You know what they say: lucky teams win cups, good teams win leagues. Big Jack was lucky in the United States."

Rhodes freely concedes that he is not a Jack Charlton fan, and he says: "A year or two ago I was at a function where Jack was speaking. He got stuck into me almost as soon as he'd been introduced. He said it had been suggested to him that the most influential referee in England since the war had been Peter Rhodes, and added that 'if you believe that, then you'll believe anything'. He was deadly serious, too, when he said it."

Rhodes told me: "I imagine that at the back of Jack's mind was the memory of the time I put Don Revie in front of an FA commission, after he had torn into Ray Tinkler, who refereed a match between Leeds United and West Brom. An Albion player broke through, and the linesman signalled that he was onside, so Tinkler let play run on, and West Brom scored. Don Revie gave Ray Tinkler some stick in public, when what he should have done was to voice his complaint in the report to the FA."

Charlton fan or not, Rhodes reckons that Big Jack - "hard, but

123

fair as a player; he wasn't a crippler" - was and is good enough to be manager of England. "He did well at club level, and if he had not chucked his hand in at Newcastle, I'm confident he would have turned things round there, as he did at Middlesbrough and Sheffield Wednesday. As for managing England, while he would have been good enough, and he would have had better material to work with, he wouldn't have fitted in with the establishment. All the time he likes to take off, to go shooting and fishing; knowing the FA, they would have had a fit!"

Ray Houghton, whose goal DID beat Italy, summed up Jack Charlton this way: "There are no stars (in the Irish camp), it does not matter if you're with Manchester United or Millwall. We're in it together. Nobody is allowed to swagger around. The lads love being in the Ireland squad; it's a great crack, and Jack has a lot to do with that. He's the big chief."

And skipper Andy Townsend talked of "a club-style atmosphere in the camp: rather than sitting around hotel rooms fretting, we have a light-hearted approach which has always worked. We do take games seriously, there's a lot at stake, but we're like a bunch of school kids after the game - when we've won. As seriously as we take the football, we all enjoy linking up with the squad because we know we'll have a good laugh, as well."

There was another insight into the kind of tactics Jack Charlton is liable to employ OFF the field of play. The Republic went to play in Albania, known throughout football as one of the most inhospitable places to go for a game of soccer, and they returned home on the right end of a 2-1 scoreline. But the players were honest enough to recognise, and admit, that they hadn't performed well.

Jack Charlton advised them to "go away and think about the match." As Ray Houghton recalled: "There were no rollickings, but when we met up again, he pulled the squad together and said, 'You were just useless in Albania, now do something about it'." Ireland "did something about it" by defeating Latvia 2-1 in Riga thus consolidating their claims to a place in the World Cup finals.

At that time, with England reeling from defeat by the United States, the knives were out for Graham Taylor with a vengeance. World Cup winner George Cohen said Taylor should be replaced. "What he seems best at is talking like the previous manager, and we've had enough of that. Alf Ramsey showed you don't need to do a lot of talking, and you should never criticise your players in public, which Taylor has done." Cohen's suggested successor: Gerry Francis, with Ray Wilkins working alongside him.

Former England skipper Johnny Haynes claimed that "the players are letting Taylor down" and suggested: "The only consolation is they may be getting it out of their system before the World Cup matches that count." And another former England captain, Billy Wright, believed that "the real question is whether we should have been playing this match at all. This trip was the last thing the players needed after a long, hard season."

Sheffield Wednesday boss Trevor Francis confirmed this reasoning when he admitted: "My own two players in the team, Chris Woods and Carlton Palmer, both need a break." And former Chelsea chairman Brian Mears, who was on the FA's international committee when it ended Sir Alf Ramsey's reign in 1974, declared: "The FA won't sack Graham Taylor. That is not the way they do things. It would take time to decide on a successor."

Meanwhile, the man more than a few folk would have backed as Taylor's successor was well on the way to taking the Republic of Ireland to the finals. That luck of the Irish had worked, also, as they had won in Lithuania to top their group. The home country were weakened by the loss of their best three players, not allowed to play by their club, Austria Vienna, because the Lithuanian F.A wouldn't or couldn't afford a £20,000 insurance premium. This despite the fact that the Spanish Football Association had offered the Lithuanians a loan.

Former Leeds United team-mate Bobby Collins reckons that Big Jack "has done better for the team than the team has done for him, by which I mean that, considering his range of choice is limited, and he hasn't got what you could call many great players, he's done wonders with the ones at his disposal. For me, the players were not as good, maybe, as some people tend to think, but Jack knows what he wants from his team, and he puts his message across so that he gets the best possible results. He was brilliant the way he steered the Republic to the finals of the 1994 World Cup, and he got the best out of his players once they had got there. He must have been a very disappointed man when he didn't get a crack at the England job, but he's gone on to prove himself in the best possible way: in effect, he's had a Scot and several Englishmen playing for the Irish. In fact, all things considered, he's done astonishingly well."

Bobby remembers his own arrival at Leeds. "Jack wasn't even in the team then - Freddie Goodwin, who was signed from Manchester United, played at centre-half - but Jack got his chance within a few weeks of my going there. And the way his career went was surprising: from the age of 18 to 28 or so, you'd have to say it was wishy-washy, but from 28 onwards he was brilliant."

Few people in football know Jack Charlton better than the man who was his trainer at international level and his right-hand man at club level, Harold Shepherdson. And he says: "Once he got something in his head, he'd take it to the end of the road. He didn't suffer fools gladly; in fact, he didn't suffer fools. He could mix with the players when he was manager at Middlesbrough but, at the same time, they all knew he was the boss. He'd got the background of having played for England, having won a World Cup medal. So he had the respect of people. He was popular, too; he would go out to places and give talks, and he could mix with the spectators. I got on very well with him at Boro' - between us, I think we had a good blend. He used to say to me, 'I'll look after the players, you look after the rest'. And he would tell me, 'When I'm not here, you'll be the boss'. Some of the players gave me the impression at times that they were frightened to death of him, but they still rated him highly. Because he'd been through the mill himself as a player, they knew that when he told you to do something, he'd been able to do it himself."

The England job? "Yes, it's a pity that he didn't manage England. One would have thought that he was the ideal man for the job. He couldn't have had a better grounding, having played under Don Revie at Leeds and Alf Ramsey with England. If he could do a good job for the Republic of Ireland, he could have done a good job here. Jack is a big man in many ways, and not just physically. We used to have loads of laughs with him when we were together in the England set-up, although he's always given the impression that he's his own man."

So what was it like to play against Jack Charlton at club level? One man who won England caps as a centre-forward, Joe Royle (he was pitched into Everton's team as a stripling of 16) answers with compete candour: "Jack wasn't above giving you a whack if you were both going for the ball, but I would never accuse him of going over the top or of using elbows. He was aggressive all right, but he was a very honest centre-half. At a time when Leeds United were not attracting the best kind of publicity for the cynical side of their game, Jack wasn't like that; he was strong, honest and fair. He wasn't one of those players who try to wind you up, and there was never anything cynical about his play."

Jack Charlton for England, as manager? Joe shrugs his own broad shoulders and answers with a question of his own. "Who can say? It's hypothetical, isn't it? What is a fact is that he's done a good job wherever he's been. I've never worked under him, but I can see him being larger than life and being quite inspirational. On that score alone he must have had a chance. Everyone who knew him said that as a player he got better as he got older."

If officials of Northern Ireland were not best pleased with their counterparts from the south, when the Republic finally arrived in the United States for the "real thing", it wasn't long before Jack Charlton was being hauled over the coals by some of the FIFA officials. They may not have said, as Peter Rhodes did, that he was "a pain in the ass" with his outspoken comments, but they certainly made their feelings plain.

One newspaper report kicked off like this: "Jack Charlton has been told to stop complaining by FIFA bosses who say they are fed up with his verbal sniping at the way the World Cup is being run". Before the tournament began, Big Jack had launched what was termed "a blistering attack on FIFA's edict restricting the way players could be given fluids during matches."

As it turned out, Charlton could claim that he was correct in making his feelings known. But the arguments raged, and they continued to rage, later on. One thing which had provoked the anger of the Republic's manager was the dope-testing of striker Tommy Coyne, who was left to sit in his soaking strip for three and a half hours before he was able to provide the required sample of urine.

Big Jack had previously remonstrated against FIFA's strictures about the way players had to go about things in order to quench their thirst during the match action. And he could claim to have forced the authorities to climb down: it was announced that water would be made available to all players, without them having to move to the touchline to get it. Jack's argument was that the touchline order was all right when it came to flank players, but it took no account of the men whose job meant they were left stranded in the middle areas of the pitch.

Charlton said: "My players trust me to take care of them. That's my prime responsibility, and I won't shirk it. Because of that concern, I had to take action on the water front. We were right to pursue it, because FIFA have changed their rules. If we'd been in the wrong, surely FIFA wouldn't have climbed down." A valid point by the Republic team boss, one would have thought.

However, FIFA general-secretary Sepp Blatter had a few pungent observations of his own to make. Like this: "If I were Mr Charlton, I would concentrate on Friday's game against Mexico and stop moaning. It's no coincidence that the only manager to complain is the one from Ireland. We've changed the rules over drinks. If his players want water they can have it. He should stop complaining."

At that stage, though, it did appear that the score so far was Jack Charlton 1, FIFA 0. Later, it was one-all as FIFA came down heavy-handed, not only on the Republic's team boss, but on the Football Association of Ireland and on John Aldridge, the striker Big Jack wanted to pitch into the fray against Mexico.

During the match, "Aldo" was on the sidelines and raring to go, but his entry on the field was delayed by an official, and Aldridge could be heard mouthing some rude words. What happened, as the Republic went down against Mexico, brought a FIFA fine of £10,000 on Jack Charlton, £1,250 on Aldridge, and £10,000 on the Football Association of Ireland. Big Jack was also banned from the touchline for the crucial final group match against Norway.

FIFA spokesman Guido Tognoni said the disciplinary committee had banned Charlton for his "constant misbehaviour during the first two games." Tognoni also declared: " We like Jack, but he's a crazy man. Football needs characters, but he must learn where to draw the line regarding his behaviour. The fines and ban have been imposed because of the overall behaviour by the Irish during the Mexico game. Jack Charlton was insulting to the FIFA co-ordinator, Egyptian Mustafa Fahmy, and the reserve officials. He also made insulting comments to the referee and linesmen. We can't punish players who show dissent and let Jack Charlton get away with it. Football is an emotional sport, and we accept that, but there is a basic standard of decorum we must expect from managers and coaches. Jack can go to the dressing-room before the Norway match, and at half-time, to talk to his players, but he can't step on to the pitch."

It was a brand of punishment which brought a massive response from Irish fans, in the shape of more than £100,000 from a "whip-round", and a telling statement from the Football Association of Ireland which read: "We are totally satisfied that the team manager and his technical staff complied fully with the procedure laid down by FIFA". The statement did not induce FIFA to relent, however, and there was no appeal against the ruling body's judgment.

American television also got into the act as it focussed on Jack Charlton's touchline behaviour. One clip showed him swearing and throwing a water container on to the track surrounding the pitch. It didn't do Big Jack's blood pressure any good; he rapped back: "It's a case of trial by television. I don't know why I've been banned for doing my job. Not one official has said anything to me. I wasn't warned by the referee about my conduct in any of the matches; I was not talked to by any of the FIFA officials. Am I entitled to a yellow card or warning? I've spent my time yelling at people to get water to my players or yelling instructions to my players from inside the touchline square. I don't understand why all this has happened. The only time we've had a problem was when we tried to get John Aldridge on to the pitch during the Mexico game."

Aldridge reckoned "FIFA are doing everything they can to get us out of the World Cup; we think we're being victimised." But even as he admitted his regret for the words he had used to Fahmy, Signor Tognoni was coming back with this: "There's no vendetta against Jack Charlton or Ireland. We know he was critical of us in the media, but that is his opinion. We have never had an official complaint from the FA of Ireland. It's disappointing, though, that in February Jack missed a seminar for managers and coaches (the point former referee Peter Rhodes had made). He was reported to be sick. Unfortunately, four years ago, before Italia '90, he missed the same kind of seminar. We feel it is important for coaches and managers to be there. It's important for them to know the guidelines."

Jack Charlton remained unabashed. "Really, I'm paying the penalty for having a go about the water situation." And, still on the theme, as he reflected upon the conditions in which teams had to play, he offered this opinion: "I don't think you can expect us to win the World Cup after what we have experienced here. I won't keep on about the heat - you'll just say I'm moaning - but, of course, it does have an effect. When it comes to playing in these conditions, we're not up to it."

Few people back home, watching the players striving to beat the hot and humid conditions as well as their opponents, would have argued with that.

An Irish War Of Words

One of the men who, as a player, received marching orders from referee Peter Rhodes, Billy Bingham, is a man I got to know pretty well. In fact, during his days as a footballer with Everton, Billy, who also had a spell with Sunderland, had a bit of a bust-up with me over a story I wrote about him, although, so far as I know, he never held a grudge, after we had agreed to disagree.

Billy's managerial career took in Southport (whom he steered to promotion when they were a League club), Plymouth Argyle and Everton, and for many years, right up to the 1994 World Cup. Indeed, he managed the Northern Ireland international team.

This former Irish international player will doubtless recall the time he signed the mercurial Duncan McKenzie, an entertainer if ever there was one. Duncan's career had its own ups and downs. For instance, he joined Jack Charlton's old club, Leeds United, though it wasn't Don Revie who signed him, but Revie's successor, Brian Clough, who got the sack after a reign of just 44 days.

Jimmy Armfield followed Clough, and he sold McKenzie to the Belgian club, Anderlecht, then Billy Bingham, installed as manager of Everton, brought Duncan back to English League football with the Goodison club. The Press conference remained vivid in McKenzie's memory, for Billy Bingham made a remark which (though neither he nor the player realised it at the time) was to prove prophetic.

As the manager and the new recruit stood side by side, Bingham put his arm around McKenzie's shoulders and, while they faced the television cameras, he cracked what seemed to be nothing more than a light-hearted quip. "The last time a manager signed you, he got the sack a couple of weeks later!" Billy was referring to the Clough episode, of course, but not many weeks after McKenzie's arrival at Everton, Bingham found himself out of a job!

During the lead-up to the 1994 World Cup finals, Billy Bingham crossed swords with Jack Charlton, after the paths of the

131

Republic and Northern Ireland had been fated to cross in the qualifying matches. When they were pitched in against each other, seldom was there a scenario for a more potentially explosive situation than the meeting of the rival teams in trouble-torn Belfast; not least, of course, because the result would have a crucial bearing upon the Republic's chances of going through to the final stages of the tournament in the United States.

When it became clear that the Northern Ireland-Republic of Ireland duel was taking on such a confrontational shape, it was suggested that the match should be switched and taken to Manchester United's Old Trafford ground, to avoid even the prospect of any trouble. All that was needed, it was being said, was for a few Ulster-based Republicans who were also football fans to produce a tricolour flag in the Windsor Park ground of Irish League club Linfield, where the needle match was scheduled to be staged, and all hell would be let loose.

While from the south there came unqualified expressions of appreciation for this clear-sighted view of what so easily could become an explosive occasion, from the north there were accusations that the Republic was simply trying to take advantage of the situation and, thereby, make Manchester United's ground what could be termed a home base for Jack Charlton's team.

And as claim and counter-claim were made, so the acrimony crept in, and with it, tempers. Finally, it was left to the footballing authorities to sort matters out and make the decision which would be binding upon both camps, and the verdict of FIFA was that the show must go on, still at Windsor Park.

There might have seemed a touch of irony in the statement from the secretary of the Irish League club, Linfield, that "the safest place in Belfast on a Saturday afternoon is inside Windsor Park." On this occasion, however, the game was being staged on a Wednesday evening, and the soccer fate of a nation could hinge upon the result. Victory for the Republic and they would be assured of a place in the finals in the United States; defeat, and their presence in those finals would be placed in jeopardy. A draw, and other results would determine Jack's fate.

It had been pointed out that the recent upsurge in violence in the province of Ulster had caused a British featherweight title fight to be switched from Belfast, and that rugby, hockey, badminton and basketball had all suffered from switches in venues or even cancellations, as teams and individuals from the Republic had decided that discretion was the better part of valour and, therefore, it would be wiser not to cross the demarcation line with the North.

As for the World Cup qualifier, it remained to be seen if Windsor Park was, indeed, "the safest place in Belfast", or if, on a Wednesday night, it turned out to be what one sportswriter termed "a target for terrorism." Five days before the event, one of the Northern Ireland players, Jimmy Quinn, had summed up his feelings in an interview which was headlined: "Giving Peace a Chance in the City that Needs to Hope". The player, it was recorded, "goes home to Belfast for a match which, he hopes, will prove that battles in his tormented homeland can be won without the need for blood to be shed. Rarely will a footballer's hope be so commonly shared. Northern Ireland's meeting with the Republic in a World Cup qualifier of momentous significance at Windsor Park will - God and the gunmen willing - be played without hurt or hindrance. There seems little doubt it will be a match staged in fear: fear from the terraces; fear inside the offices of FIFA, who allowed it to proceed; and fear for the citizens who live down the road on Shankhill, where so much innocent life has been taken across the years. There will not, though, be fear on the field." So said the report.

To Quinn the player, it was "just another game", his 37th for his country. But, obviously, it was far from being just another game, for himself and for many others. As the sportswriter wrote: "A win for the men of Ulster will deny the Republic the place in the United States they had begun to take for granted. The Republic have never won in Belfast; the boys from the North will not be scared, they never are. Even the upsurge in violence that has scarred the streets recently will not deter them."

Jimmy Quinn said: "They were talking about taking the game away from Belfast, but that could never have happened. I didn't believe they'd move it. There has been trouble before. I remember a game against England a few years back was stopped for half an hour because the police heard that mortars were being aimed at the ground. Nothing happened. For the people of Northern Ireland, a game like this is an escape. They love their football, they love all sports, as much as anyone else. A lot of people in the North were rooting for the lads in the Republic when they reached the finals in 1990. I don't think they will be on Wednesday night, mind."

He added: "I can't imagine why anyone would want to cause

trouble this week - from our point of view, all we want to do is play hard and hope we win. It's a fascinating game, because of the different styles of the two sides. We play more football. We have a passing game, though the Republic's style, we know, is more direct. But there are plenty of players in their side who know about knocking the ball around."

This particular football match was described by one writer in terms which demonstrated just how seriously people viewed the situation, overall. "Any match between Northern Ireland and the Republic carries the potential for tribal conflict. But a match played at such a time, at such a venue, and with so much at stake, raises the forthcoming contest to a hazardous level of intensity."

To be certain of qualifying for the World Cup finals, the Republic had to win, and while victory for Northern Ireland would leave them with "nothing more than the satisfaction of having scuppered the dreams of their neighbours," this in itself was "a prize they dearly covet." To add spice to the occasion, the match would be the swan-song for Northern Ireland's manager, Billy Bingham, and he could be certain that his players would be doing their level best to give him a farewell victory salute.

The Republic's football authority, the Football Association of Ireland, had to withstand accusations of having made "ham-fisted" efforts to get the match switched from Belfast. It was reported that the association had sent a delegation to a FIFA meeting in Zurich 'to drop clumping hints about the new levels of violence in the Province, and how much better things would be if the two Irelands could settle their argument on neutral territory, preferably Manchester, but anywhere other than Windsor Park."

And the claim was made: "These machinations had nothing to do with a fear of playing in Belfast, but everything to do with seizing an advantage. Any game outside the Six Counties would be effectively a home game for the Republic, so desperate are their fans to see them qualify."

It was further recorded that, for a brief space of time, the officials of FIFA appeared to be amenable to a switch of venue, and that travel agents in Dublin had taken out options on more than 5,000 aircraft seats, while at Manchester United's headquarters, Old Trafford, a meeting had been held to finalise catering arrangements for the big match, if it were to be staged there.

As for the Irish Football Association (the North's counterpart of the FAI), should such an event take place, it would receive compensation from profits approaching half a million pounds, and, since the IFA coffers were not exactly overflowing, it was confidently anticipated they would not turn up their noses at the prospect of such a bonanza.

But the Irish Football Association dug its heels in and said the game must go on at Windsor Park. As one of the security officials put it: "This is our World Cup final." The IFA did have a little help from its opponents, too, because the Republic declined to take up its allocation of tickets (which, in any event, amounted to no more than 400 for the match). Even so, this didn't mean there would be no Republican sympathisers at the game and, as a Linfield-club steward was quoted as saying: "If there's a load of fellers waving Union Jacks and yet another feller pulls out a Free State tricolour, well, we'd have to make decisions."

The Republic of Ireland manager and his players had hoped to make it a quick in-and-out job, but it was decreed that they would now arrive on the day before the match, spend most of their waiting hours resting in an hotel, then play the World Cup-tie and head back for Dublin immediately afterwards. The plan was that win, lose or draw, they would be back on southern territory before the clock chimed the hour of midnight. Whether it would be to celebrate success, or to hold what might be considered a wake, remained to be seen.

Another intriguing aspect of the all-Irish confrontation was that on the continent of Europe that same day, Spain would be meeting Denmark. Denmark were not only the European champions, they were also at the head of their World Cup group, with Spain lying second and the Republic in third place. Northern Ireland had already blown their chance, they were playing for pride.

The kick-off time of both matches was the same, 8p.m., and news of what was happening at Windsor Park would be relayed to the combatants in Seville. One of Denmark's players, Michael Laudrup, was prompted to forecast that "our game against Spain may well turn into a no-contest", on the basis that "if we hear the game in Belfast is a draw, or the Republic are losing, the Spanish players will not want to do anything too risky against us. They'll be concerned about taking chances, in case we hit them on the break." So the ball would stay around the middle of the field, "and

I'd imagine the Spanish will be happy to play out time. That's fine by us - as long as we get to the finals."

The Republic of Ireland players (never having won in Ulster) knew that if they did no better than draw, Denmark would have to beat Spain, or Spain would have to win by at least two clear goals, in order for Jack Charlton's men to reach the finals. So the situation was balanced on a knife-edge as the four sides prepared for their make-or-break encounters. One of the Northern Ireland players, Jim Magilton, confirmed: "There's no way we'll be holding anything back; if the Republic want a place in the finals, they'll have to earn it."

Ironically, Alan Kernaghan, one of the men in the Republic's hybrid squad, had been born in England, reared in Northern Ireland, and had actually played for the Northern Ireland schoolboy side. When he lived in Bangor, County Down, he used to go with his pals to watch the big soccer games in Belfast

Kernaghan admitted that at that stage in his life, his ambition had been to play for Northern Ireland at senior level. But although both his grandparents had been born in Belfast, this didn't qualify him to play for Northern Ireland. Later, the regulations were changed, so he would then have had a genuine qualification to play for Northern Ireland, but by the time this had come about, he had taken up another option, one which allowed him to wear the green jersey of the Republic of Ireland.

So he said: "My days as a Northern Ireland fan and all the memories are history now; the tables have been turned, and I'm now in a position where I must do something for myself. The lads I used to go with to the games at Windsor Park think I should be playing for their team and will be only too willing to rub it in, if we lose."

Kernaghan described the match as "like a cup final: a massive prize is at stake. This could prove to be my one and only chance of reaching the finals." And when his playing days were over? "I think of Bangor as home, because my family still live there, and it's my wife's home town, too. I would eventually like to live in Ireland, whether it's north or south of the border remains to be seen."

So Kernaghan and his team-mates arrived for the match amid a massive security operation, having been refused permission to stay south of the border in County Monaghan and travel straight to

Windsor Park by coach. Thus they were taken to their hideaway hotel (the venue had been changed four times) escorted by no fewer than half a dozen armoured personnel carriers. Meanwhile, all roads between the airport and the hotel had been sealed off, as part of the security operation.

Jack Charlton summed up the situation as he pointed out: "We have to go to Dublin to fly to Belfast and be there 24 hours before the game. It's going to take half a day for a journey that would have taken us an hour and a quarter by coach, but we'll do whatever we're told."

One correspondent who intended to go to the game wrote about "the eerie conditions imposed upon it by the recent murderous attacks in this beleaguered capital. Merely to get to Windsor Park was to know the city's suffering: the boarded-up windows of abandoned houses, the obscene tribal threats on walls."

The security plans for the night of the match included the introduction of a "sterile" area extending for the best part of a mile in a circle around the Windsor Park ground - anyone who wanted to get through the cordon of troops and police would have to present a valid ticket for the game - and the fans could expect to face constant checks, as officials sought to make sure that no-one tried to pass off a forgery, or anything more sinister.

Troops, members of the Royal Ulster Constabulary, armoured vehicles and plain-clothes members of the security services were in position and detailed to block off the side roads and create what amounted to a ring of steel. So many were there on duty that for every four of the 10,000 soccer fans going to the game, there was at least one person keeping a watchful eye on them. Close on 3,000 men were on the alert to ensure that trouble did not flare up before, during, or after the match.

On the very eve of the match, the rival managers had a verbal brush as Billy Bingham offered, as his opinion, that a lot of the players on the Republic team were happy to be chosen "because they couldn't find a way to making it with England or Scotland." Bingham, indeed, declared that the Republic's team was made up of "football mercenaries", a barb which incensed Jack Charlton, who countered: "What am I to do - ignore a damn good player with Irish parents just because he happens to have been born in the UK?"

Bingham declared: "I take a totally cynical view of the entire business, although it's for others to judge whether the Republic are actually devaluing the World Cup." Players on the Republic side were astonished by the outburst, and one, John Aldridge, indignantly retorted: "Calling us mercenaries is garbage." In his view, what the Northern Ireland manager had said was "nothing short of scandalous, a disgrace." The player added: "When I was first picked for Ireland, I didn't see pound notes before my eyes. I saw shamrocks. My pedigree is Irish, so is my patriotism, and it hurts whenever anyone questions it."

Jack Charlton also counter-attacked, as he said: "In building my Irish squad I've had to stick strictly within the rules of FIFA. Every one of my Republic players has been approved by them and the Irish Government. Northern Ireland, England and the rest have the right to recruit players on the same basis as us. My squad building has been not so much a policy as a necessity."

Overnight, the city of Belfast saw media personnel flooding in, and many of them were from American television. They could sense "a story of some magnitude", so it was said - a story not about a World Cup match, but one which concerned "whether the occasion will be seized upon by insane intractable terrorists to focus world attention on Belfast." David Bowen, secretary of the Irish Football Association, declared: "Some of the television crews who have come over from America make no bones about the story they are looking for, even hoping for."

While it was being said that Belfast "needs this match like a stray bullet in the head", one commentator was putting it another way, like this: "The issue is devastatingly simple. If the Republic of Ireland win, they will proceed to next Summer's World Cup finals, a venture worth minimally £5 million to football in the Republic and £100,000 to each of its international players. If Northern Ireland win, they will win nothing but an academic football match - they will simply have blocked the Republic's path to vast prosperity."

And so it came to pass that more than 10,000 people flocked to Windsor Park to witness what was, by any standards, an acknowledged, "supremely tense sporting occasion", a one-off drama in which no-one knew for certain if the game of soccer would get through its allotted 90 -minute span of action on the field without the accompaniment of bombs or bullets being sprayed around.

In the event, the match passed off amid an explosion of sound caused by the cheers of those supporting the Republic, who gained an honourable draw, after having gone behind with fewer than 20 minutes remaining. When the Republic equalised, shortly afterwards, it was the first goal they had ever scored while playing in Belfast. And the result from Spain (the home country won 1-0) meant that the Spaniards finished on top of the group, with the Republic and Denmark lying joint second. So the Republic got the trip to America by virtue of having scored more goals in their group matches than Denmark had done.

Qualifiers

WORLD CUP FINALS 1994
in the United States of America

Qualifiers:

Argentina, Belgium, Bolivia, Brazil, Bulgaria, Cameroon, Colombia, Germany, Greece, Holland, Italy, Mexico, Morocco, Nigeria, Norway, REPUBLIC OF IRELAND, Romania, Russia, Saudi Arabia, South Korea, Spain, Sweden, Switzerland, United States.

Notable absentees:
ENGLAND, SCOTLAND, NORTHERN IRELAND.

Republic of Ireland - Results
GROUP E
Italy 0, Republic of Ireland 1 (Houghton - 11 minutes).
Attendance 73,511.
Republic of Ireland 1 (Aldridge - 84 minutes), Mexico 2 (Garcia - 42 & 66 minutes). Attendance 61,219.
Republic of Ireland 0, Norway 0. Attendance 76,322.

	P	W	D	L	F	A	Pts
Mexico	3	1	1	1	3	3	4
Republic of Ireland	3	1	1	1	2	2	4
Italy	3	1	1	1	2	2	4
Norway	3	1	1	1	1	1	4

LAST SIXTEEN
Holland 2 (Bergkamp - 11 minutes, Jonk - 41 minutes),
Republic of Ireland 0
Attendance 61,355

* There were 227 bookings during the tournament and 15 players sent off. The total of goals scored was 141, an average of 2.7 a game.

Seeing Stars

Twenty-two players, and while some of them spoke with genuine Irish accents, others conversed in a dialect which marked them down as native Scousers or even Glaswegian. Yet Jack Charlton got them all together and welded them into a fighting force which won nothing but admiration for him and them from the fans who followed the Republic of Ireland to the World Cup finals in 1994.

During those finals, a couple of them, Jason McAteer and Phil Babb, saw their value in the transfer market soar to heights of which they could only have dreamed a few months previously. McAteer, 22 years old and beginning to make his mark with home-spun Bolton Wanderers, and Babb, still only 23 years of age and a player who earned his living with one of the Premiership's unfashionable clubs, Coventry City.

I watched young Babb when he was playing for Bradford City in the Third Division, after he had done a stint with Millwall. I must confess that then I didn't see him as someone who would win his spurs in competition with the greatest names in world football.

Bobby Collins, who, like myself, had seen a fair bit of Babb while he wore the colours of the Valley Parade club recalls: "He played at left-back and left-half then, and I always regarded him as a very steady player. He didn't have many bad games. But since he joined Coventry and got his chance as a World Cup centre-back with the Republic of Ireland, he's fairly blossomed."

Babb went to the World Cup with four caps under his belt, while McAteer, whose family name had earlier been more famed in boxing circles, had played five times for the Republic. He had been persuaded to turn his back on the chance to opt for England or Northern Ireland.

By the time he was chosen for the trip to the United States, he was said to be on the brink of ousting Ray Houghton, the experienced and much-travelled midfielder who played for Aston Villa, after having won so many honours while with Liverpool. In the event, Houghton kept his place for the most part, and did a switch, while McAteer paraded his footballing talents as a right-sided play-er who had a brain in his head as well as skill in his boots.

Babb, meanwhile, formed an extremely competent partnership with Paul McGrath, who helped to nurse the younger man along even as Babb gained experience himself from match to match. One of the attributes that Babb possessed was a very real turn of speed, and, like McAteer, he showed that he could work things out on the park as well.

Before they returned home from America, they were to learn that together they were being valued at no less than £5M as poten-tial targets for the big clubs in the Premiership. Liverpool, for one, were being linked with them. It was said that Coventry were reject-ing all overtures for Babb - also coveted by Tottenham Hotspur - and that the bidding was certain to continue up to £3M or more.

McAteer celebrated his 23rd birthday on the day the Irish beat Italy in their group game, and Aston Villa manager Ron Atkinson, over in the States to do a spot of TV commentating, had the chance, personally, to monitor the progress of the lad from Merseyside. What was said to have impressed Big Ron was the mature manner in which McAteer, who preferred a central midfield role, had per-formed as a wide man on the right.

McAteer revealed: "I've found it easier to break into the team here because I've had lads like Phil (Babb) and Gary Kelly to help me settle in. If I'd been a young player left on my own, it might have been a lot harder." Giving credit where it was due, also, McAteer said: "I've learned a lot from Bolton manager Bruce Rioch and coach Colin Todd. I appreciate the education they've given me. I just hope that eventually I can play against the best players in England, week in, week out."

Babb's reaction to finding fame thrust upon him? "I feel I'm a better all-round player, and that should stand me in good stead." Like Jason McAteer, Phil Babb could feel pretty confident that before too long, his club would have to listen to the big-money bids. As, indeed, they did, when Liverpool paid more than £3.5M.

When the Republic of Ireland came up against Italy, Babb was facing the greatest challenge of his career: he had to try to curb the attacking menace that was Roberto Baggio. It says much for Babb's belief in himself, as he prepared to line up for this World Cup opener, that he expressed his confidence not only in his abili-ty, but in his style of play.

"People have told me that I'm too laid-back and lazy, but I haven't changed over the years. I'm naturally like that. Even so, I always give 100 per cent, and would never shirk anything. I'll have Paul McGrath out there alongside me, and you can't find anybody more laid-back than him."

Five years previously, Babb had kicked off as an 18-year-old with Millwall, so he had come a long way in a short space of time, and he admitted as much when he said: "I can't imagine what it will be like, stepping out against the Italians. I'm trying not to think about it; I don't want the whole aura surrounding the game hitting me, in case I'm overawed. But I can't wait to face players like Baggio, Donadoni and Signori. It's the kind of game you dream about being involved in, and I want to show everyone that I can live with the best."

The Republic claimed their first and most notable scalp, with their 1-0 victory over Italy, and Phil Babb, like Jason McAteer, was on his way to stardom. At that time, there were some worries about Roy Keane's fitness, and Jack Charlton criticised Manchester United's £3.7M player for having failed to report an injury earlier. He had trained for two days at the team's base in Orlando before revealing the extent of the problem, and Big Jack said: "I'm not very pleased about that."

Later in the tournament, Charlton paraded Keane and assistant manager Maurice Setters before a Press conference, the object of the exercise being to kill off rumours of a training-ground flare-up between Setters and the player. The rumours had circulated about there being friction between Setters and several players, not just Keane, during an extra session of training while the manager was away in Miami watching group rivals Mexico in action.

That little matter satisfactorily disposed of, it was back to football, and it was Paul McGrath who came into the firing line, after what, for him, was a disappointing performance in the defeat by Mexico. Jack Charlton then talked of dropping his star defender.

Big Jack revealed: "I consulted with Andy Townsend and Kevin Moran, who know him well, and they advised that Paul often responds to a kick up the backside. I waited until the day of the game against Norway before deciding I would play him, but I retained the option of substituting him, and I would have used it, if necessary."

Charlton went so far as to take McGrath to one side during a training session and quiz him about his attitude. McGrath, whose display against Italy had been described by team-mate Andy Townsend as "awesome", was desperate not to miss out on the action later, and he insisted that he was prepared to play, as the Irish made their "last stand" against Norway.

He was suffering from what his manager called "a dead leg", and it was left until the morning of the match. Then "we'll let Paul decide." In the event, McGrath played, and he did himself and his team proud. Charlton had stung him, all right, when he said: "He was brilliant against Italy, a long way below his best against Mexico. If we hadn't been behind, and the urgent need had not been for offensive players, I would have brought him off."

Jack Charlton himself talked about the psychology he employed to get the best out of a world-class defender who, it was reported, "so often teeters on the brink of self-destruction." It was said that the Republic's manager appeared happy to accommodate stars and was big enough to make exceptions. For example, McGrath had been restored to the squad immediately after he had pulled out of a game against Albania without apparent reason.

At 34, McGrath was obviously coming to the close of his foot-balling career, rather than being in the first flush of youth, and he was said to have "admitted to having problems in the past curbing his alcohol intake and overcoming the wear and tear of a succession of knee injuries that have left him with arthritis. But his ability as a footballer ensures he receives special consideration from his managers, at club and country level."

By the time the 1994 World Cup came along, McGrath had won 65 caps and had recently signed a new "pay-as-you-play" contract at Aston Villa. In suggesting that McGrath might be dropped from international duty for the first time, Jack Charlton knew his man: the defender would be hurt, even at the thought.

Charlton himself confirmed: "Right up to finally picking the team (for the game against Mexico) Paul was an issue in my mind. Sometimes there are ways to handle him. You have to put him under a bit of pressure; you need to use a bit of psychology. Andy Townsend pointed out that at Aston Villa Paul will do no training all week, then, by the Saturday, their manager, Ron Atkinson, will say he won't use Paul. But then Ron will suddenly change his mind and play him. In those circumstances, Paul does fine. There was intentional psychology in the build-up to the Norway game with

Paul.

"I asked him on the morning of the game how he felt. He said he was all right. I asked him if he wanted to play, whether he could get through it OK. He assured me he could. It was then I told him he could play and, to be fair, he did fine. Had he said no to me, I would have played Alan Kernaghan, who is a very fit young lad. But as long as Paul reads the game and plays like he did against Norway, everything is fine."

It was indicative of the team spirit that Jack Charlton had built up, also, that Kernaghan, a £1.5M signing by Manchester City, backed the boss's decision, saying: "Jack was going to pull Paul off and send me on against Mexico, which surprised me; I thought Paul had done quite well. He wasn't to blame for either of the goals, and although I would love to play, I don't see how Paul can go from being the world's best player against Italy and then be left out of the team."

One of the things which Jack Charlton had talked about, before he and his men went into the World Cup finals, was his fears about them "living in a goldfish bowl". "I worry about all the attention. For instance, I will allow the players at the right moments to have a drink; they may even be allowed out to a local bar in Florida or New York. I'm concerned, though, that some sections of the media may try to exploit that and create a story that doesn't really exist."

In point of fact, his players decided to forego a trip to Disneyworld at a time when they felt they would be better resting and preparing for the next battle on the field of play. So they showed they had their priorities right. Then came the fines imposed on Big Jack, John Aldridge and the Football Association of Ireland. Now here was a BIG story.

It was indeed big enough for a television crew to decide it was worth their while to confront Jack and his players when they arrived at their hotel, but they discovered that instead of getting pictures of the manager, he was thrusting his hand in front of their cameras and, clearly not in the best of humours, marching past and into the hotel.

It was a tense time for Charlton and his men, as everyone waited to see if they would be needled enough to commit any indiscretion. In fact, John Aldridge made a public apology for his behaviour on the touchline, admitting he had been "out of order" in bad-mouthing the official who impeded him from going on as a substitute against Mexico.

When he did get into the action, with the score 2-0, "Aldo" struck to give the Irish a fighting chance. As he said: "It's funny how things work out. My goal got us through, yet at the time I thought it was just a consolation. As it worked out, it was priceless." Aldridge, a Scouser who had scored goals galore at club level from Newport to Oxford United to Liverpool, not to mention Real Sociedad, had often appeared a player with something to prove in Jack Charlton's tactical scheme of things with the Republic of Ireland. Yet he never complained, taking the rough with the smooth and always doing his level best to fit in and carry on with his job - which meant getting on the end of things and scoring goals, as he was then doing for Tranmere Rovers at club level.

At 35, he went into the 1994 World Cup with 13 goals in 58 outings to his credit, and he believed he still had two more years' worth of goals inside him. When the Republic played Latvia, he was a hat-trick marksman, and the man who had struck a record-equalling total of 40 goals for Tranmere Rovers could point to more than 400 League games and more than 270 goals at club level. Had Niall Quinn been fit for the World Cup, it is possible that he and Aldridge would have formed the first-choice strike formation.

As it was, Jack Charlton turned to Motherwell's Tommy Coyne, a 31-year-old with four goals in 14 international games. Coyne had been no more than an occasional substitute, but he was a hero in a 1-0 victory over Holland before the World Cup finals, and he ran himself into the ground during the win over Italy.

As the team flew back to Orlando and the steamy heat of Florida, he was taken ill - feeling the effects of dehydration - and for much of the two-and-a-half-hour trip he had to lie on the floor of the aircraft, being helped down from the plane on arrival. Meanwhile, another of Big Jack's strike force, the six-foot-tall Tony Cascarino (who returned from the World Cup to be given a free transfer by Chelsea and a one-year contract by Marseille), was demonstrating yet again how much the players wanted to be a part of it all.

Cascarino, troubled by injury even before the finals kicked off, just refused an easy get-out when offered the opportunity of a return home. Cascarino, aged 31 and with a dozen goals and 50 caps behind him, decided to soldier on, and he got his belated reward with an appearance in the final match, as the Irish strove manfully to come from behind against Holland.

The striker had torn a calf muscle in the very first week of the acclimatisation training in Orlando, but he made it clear where his loyalties lay when he said: "Jack asked me if I wanted to go home. I said 'no'. I'm a lot better than I was when we started, but I won't be physically fit for a while. I don't want to go back, and six months down the line when somebody asks me what I did in the World Cup I'll have to admit, 'nothing'. I prayed we would get through the qualifying group and I'd be part of the knock-out phase. There's no way Jack can start me against Holland - I haven't trained for three weeks - but I hope he will use me for shock tactics in another game." That opportunity never arose, but at least Cascarino had the consolation of being able to say: "I played in the finals of the World Cup." This one was the second time around for him, and he admitted: "I won't be around for the next one."

That was the almost-certain fate of midfield man Ray Houghton, as well, a hero who scored the goal which took the Republic to victory in their opening match against one of the eventual finalists, Italy. Houghton's success story is an interesting one, because, as he once told me, he would have given his right arm to play for Scotland, at one stage. Now, at 32, he could look back on 58 international appearances with the Republic, and a regular place in their games in the finals. But it might well never have been like that.

For a footballer who was handed a free transfer, Houghton hasn't done badly, although he did admit to me that when he was allowed to leave West Ham, after having made just one League appearance, it was a shattering blow. "My worst moment in the game" was how he described it, adding: "The more so, since I felt I'd been playing well and had scored 17 goals that season in the reserves. Being given a free was a shock to the system."

But the best moments were yet to come: playing for the Republic, scoring for a Milk Cup-winning side at Wembley (when Oxford United beat Queen's Park Rangers), winning honours galore with Liverpool, and commanding near-£1M transfer fees when he joined the Anfield club and then Aston Villa (who defeated Manchester United in another Cup final at Wembley).

Born in Glasgow, Ray Houghton is the son of an Irishman who played in Scottish junior football. His Dad could operate in a dual role, because he played up front or at centre-half. The Houghton family moved to London when Ray was 10, but by that time he had already become a fan of Glasgow Celtic, having watched them on TV when they won the European Cup.

Ray Houghton had a school pal called Dennis Phillips, who was spotted by a West Ham scout. The scout asked Phillips if he knew of any other lads with soccer potential, and that was how Houghton's name cropped up. He and his pal were team-mates in a Sunday side. And so he joined West Ham, where he spent three years before being given a free.

At that time Reading had their eyes on him, but when he returned from a holiday it was to find the manager of another club, Fulham, waiting for him at the airport. The manager was Malcolm Macdonald, known to Newcastle and Arsenal fans as "Supermac" during his days as a scoring centre-forward, and so Houghton became a Fulham player. Three years there, and he was on his way to Oxford, then to Liverpool. And by 1990 he had become a key player in Jack Charlton's Irish international team.

Four years later, he had joined Aston Villa for £1M, but by the time the World Cup finals in America came around, he was facing what one paper termed "a tough battle from the younger squad members to hang on to his place." Indeed, like Paul McGrath, Houghton felt the sting of Charlton's tongue.

The Republic of Ireland manager was wondering - and he said as much - if Houghton were still as committed and competitive as he had been, and this rankled with the Villa midfield man. He was sufficiently stung, indeed, once he had learned that he would be in the team to meet Italy, to show he could still deliver the goods, and, as events proved, he was the Republic's match-winner.

He said afterwards: "When Jack questioned whether I was hungry enough, it hurt me. I hope it was all a wind-up by Jack. Whenever I'm on the field I give 100 per cent. If I don't, I don't deserve to be playing. I'm just pleased I gave my answer against Italy."

And while he was able to bask in the satisfaction of knowing he had played such a significant role for his side, his Aston Villa team-mate, Paul McGrath, derived equal satisfaction from hearing an opponent - Paolo Maldini (voted one of Italy's heroes as they went on to reach the final) - say of him: "McGrath was world-class, as good a centre-back as I've ever seen." Coming from such an accomplished player as Maldini, who was the recipient of many bouquets himself, this was praise, indeed.

When the Republic went to Italy for the finals of the World Cup in 1990, and reached the quarter-finals of the competition, they had Mick McCarthy as their captain, a centre-half in the Jack Charlton mould. By 1994, McCarthy was the manager of Millwall and strongly tipped to succeed Charlton as team boss of the Republic of Ireland, whenever Big Jack decided to let go the reins.

Yorkshire-born, and in his mid-thirties, McCarthy has become close to the Republic's manager, and after Big Jack had been fined £10,000 by FIFA, McCarthy expressed his confidence that Charlton would not be put off seeing his side maintain their challenge at the game's highest level. "Everyone is hurt by criticism," McCarthy said. "But Jack is his own man and won't be swayed by outside influences. He just walks away from his critics. Jack's secret is that his players trust him. He looks after his boys; he's very loyal. He must have thought long and hard about Paul McGrath and Ray Houghton before criticising them in the build-up to the finals. It was the first time I'd heard him take this approach, but you could say it has worked. Jack always put the team first. When I played for him there were times when everybody wanted to have a go at me, but he took the flak away. He has done the same for other lads in similar situations. The spirit in the camp is bigger than any individual, but the greatest individual is Jack. He gets a bigger cheer than his players from the fans, and they're happy about that. He takes the pressure off them. It's a fun team to be with - there hasn't been a clique since Jack started. Initially, there was: lads used to arrive in Dublin and go off to see their families, but he changed that. They'll have a pint on Monday, a trip to the cinema on Tuesday. It was good crack, and I miss that more than the football. The Irish camaraderie is a legend in football. If you don't like what Jack stands for, you don't turn up. He believes that if you want to voice an opinion, you can voice it from Manchester or London, but not in Dublin. He once made a decision to drop Liam Brady, and although he took stick he was completely unmoved. That's the way he is; you can't bend him."

Of the squad which went to the 1994 World Cup finals, there was a handful of genuine, home-produced Irishmen, along with a bunch of other players whose accents varied considerably. Steve Staunton, born in Drogheda; Ronnie Whelan, from Dublin; Paul

McGrath, born in Ealing (though signed by Manchester United from St. Patrick's Athletic); Ray Houghton, born in Glasgow; David Kelly, born in Birmingham; John Aldridge and Jason McAteer, from Liverpool; Roy Keane, from Cork; Phil Babb, born in Lambeth; Terry Phelan, born in Manchester; Denis Irwin, born in Cork.

Put together, however, they all formed a squad which had a genuine family feeling about it, and if some of the players didn't get into the action as often as they would have liked (or even at all, for that matter), it made no difference. Kevin Moran, capped 71 times, was 38 years old, and he went along for the ride, as events turned out. Ronnie Whelan, at 32 and with 50 caps, was in and out of the side, as the occasion demanded. So was David Kelly, a striker who found himself pitched in against the Dutch, in that desperate pursuit of a goal during the final match involving the Republic.

Kelly had notched seven goals in his 16 previous international appearances, and it was recorded that he had shown great loyalty in turning up for duty, "even if the best he can hope for is a place among the substitutes." And this despite his record of having the best goals-per-game ratio of Jack Charlton's strike force. It was also recorded how Big Jack had made it his business to make Kelly feel wanted, to the point where he heaped praise upon the striker almost every time he touched the ball when he was playing for his club side, which, as it happened, was Newcastle United at the time.

By then, Jack Charlton was doing a stint as a commentator for ITV, and it was on the final day of season 1992-93. The match in question was being played between Newcastle United and Leicester City, at St. James' Park, and Leicester were overwhelmed, 7-1.

Kelly, like some of the other footballers in Jack Charlton's Irish squad, has travelled around a bit in his search for fame, as well as goals (Walsall, West Ham, Leicester City, Newcastle United, and by the Summer of 1994 he was with Wolves) - but to hear Jack Charlton talk, during the Newcastle-Leicester match, you could have been forgiven for thinking that here was the answer to every manager's prayer: a marksman extraordinaire.

In fact, during his spell with Leicester Kelly was heading for a career total of a century of goals, although more than 60 of them had come while he was playing for Walsall, who sold him to West Ham for £600,000. By the time he joined Leicester, the fee had been halved.

However, in that final match of the season at St. James' Park, David Kelly was not outshone by a player who had cost the Magpies £1.75M, Andy Cole. Like Cole, he was a hat-trick hero in the demolition job Newcastle did on Leicester. That season Cole totalled a dozen goals in as many appearances, while Kelly contributed two dozen goals in his 45 games. And by 1994, he was playing in the finals of the World Cup, even if he had only a bit part amid the action.

When it comes to other players in the squad, and the prospect of the 1996 European championships, Jack Charlton has some major decisions to make, as he scans through the list of those who are qualified to play for the Republic of Ireland. Some of his 1994 squad will certainly be past their sell-by-date, should the Republic reach the finals, while others will remain eligible, both on the score of age, as well as ability.

Plainly, however, some new faces must be found to reinforce the squad, just as players like Phil Babb and Jason McAteer were introduced for the 1994 World Cup finals. But as Jack Charlton and his merry men returned from the United States and headed for Dublin to enjoy the acclaim of the massed thousands who now follow the Republic as if drawn by a Pied Piper, there was a bit of breathing space and time to reflect upon past glories, if only briefly. One of the great things about it all was the manner in which, in addition to having welded a bunch of footballers into a family, Big Jack had created an Irish fan club that many other countries (not least England) would surely envy.

Not only are there many thousands of them in Ireland, the Republic left a lot more behind in the States. One New York cop to whom I talked was one of these, and he spoke with genuine pride about being a supporter of Jack Charlton's team. Naturally, it helped that originally he had crossed the Atlantic from the Emerald Isle, Dublin to be precise.

The Charlton view of the fans? He made that clear when he said: "The Irish fans love a party, and they behave themselves. They made friends from other countries at the last World Cup and at the European championships in Germany in 1988. The fans will capture the imagination of the Americans."

Well, it remains to be seen if the citizens of the United States take soccer to their hearts, once the 1994 World Cup has been consigned to the history books, but it will indeed be a long time before they forget that it was party time, and that the Irish supporters made the most of it.

World Cup Woe

Jack Charlton showed his displeasure with FIFA even before he became embroiled in the arguments over drinking water for the players and the battle to get John Aldridge on the field as a substitute against Mexico. Indeed, he warned that there could be chaos, and accused FIFA of risking confusion on the pitch by the way football's ruling body had tampered with the laws of the game.

Big Jack charged: "The game is being run by people who have not got a clue about the needs of players and teams." FIFA had ordered the referees and linesmen to act decisively when it came to penalising the tackle from behind, and to give attacking players the benefit of the doubt in offside situations. Jack Charlton claimed: "It's ludicrous - they've told the referees, but nobody has told us yet. Coaches are the men responsible for preparing their players properly, and we are not in a proper position to tell them what to do. I don't know what they mean when they talk about a red card for a tackle from behind. There are loads of different challenges from behind where the ball can be won cleanly. And what is the point in schooling players to push up and clear their 18-yard area if the opposition attackers they leave behind are not going to be penalised for offside? We're talking about the World Cup, the peak of football, and suddenly people want to make fundamental changes to some of the rules when we're playing in the finals. If this is what they wanted, they should have been doing it all the way through the qualification stages. It has taken 100 years to get the rules so that everybody could understand them, now they're making them more vague.

"All this does is cause unnecessary aggravation with the players on the field. Coaches will find a way of exploiting the situation. What I have said might get me into trouble, but, then again, it might prompt them to send all the coaches a video illustrating exactly what we can and cannot do. The job of a referee is difficult enough, without such an unnecessary burden being heaped upon them in this World Cup."

The chairman of FIFA's referees' committee, David Wills (a Scot), made the point that "we have tried, by changing the psychology of referees, to take away the advantage of the defenders and give it to the attackers." And in the event, while some referees found themselves being phased out and catching the plane home, after the initial flurry of protests and arguments about the spate of yellow cards being produced, people generally settled down and accepted that this was the way things were going to be.

There were no complaints about the way the Republic of Ireland players went into action, even if two of them, Terry Phelan and Denis Irwin, were ruled out of the game against Norway. And there were no complaints from the Irish fans when their team returned home, even after having virtually gifted two goals to the Dutch. Before he set off for the United States, Big Jack said: "I just want the Irish people to be able to remain proud of a team who are recognised as a force in world football." That they were; he got his wish.

The Republic could not have chosen a tougher opening assignment than their reunion with Italy in New York. Twice the countries had met before, and twice Italy had conquered the Irish, albeit by a close margin each time. Now Jack Charlton claimed: "They won't relish meeting us, in fact, no-one in America will be comfortable playing against the Irish." Even Holland, their ultimate conquerors, were to admit beforehand that they expected a difficult ride.

Certainly Italy were stunned by the early goal which Ray Houghton scored, as he capitalised on a hesitant defence when Franco Baresi, captain of the three-times World Cup winners, headed the ball close by the Republic's midfielder. Houghton chested the ball down, took one further stride, then sent a lofted shot goalwards, and, with 'keeper Gianluca Pagliuca stranded off his line, there could be only one result. The ball sailed over him and into the net.

Whether it was a piece of supreme soccer skill or whether it was the luck of the Irish, it made no difference. The Republic had their tails up, and they denied the Italians time and space, so that even the great Roberto Baggio could not master the defenders. In eight years, the Republic had lost only five times in competitive matches, and, once ahead, they were not about to lose this one.

Houghton almost did some damage again, with little more than

20 minutes to go, as he forced Pagliuca to make a fine save, then the Aston Villa man bowed out, making way for Bolton's Jason McAteer, who was celebrating his 23 birthday. Still the Republic presented problems for the Italians, and John Sheridan saw one effort strike the crossbar, while Andy Townsend brought a diving save from the 'keeper.

For Italy, this defeat was a stunner: not once in a dozen previous opening World Cup-final games had they finished up on the losing end. They had also won in all their seven previous meetings with the Republic of Ireland. Now, it was the turn of Jack Charlton's men to laugh, even if Terry Phelan, Denis Irwin and Tommy Coyne had all seen the referee brandish the yellow card for what, back home, would scarcely have been deemed an offence at all.

No matter; the Republic of Ireland had made up for their quarter-final defeat against Italy four years previously, and the result meant that they were well on their way to qualifying from their group to the knock-out stages of the competition. Already, the future of the Italian coach, Arrigo Sacchi, was being called into question, although he was to experience the thrill of taking his team right through to the final and into a penalty shoot-out with Brazil, before the World Cup was over.

Meanwhile, so far as the Irish were concerned, it was a case of "Bring on the Mexicans" but to meet them, the players and manager of the Republic had to travel from New York to Orlando, in Florida, where they would confront Mexico in the Citrus Bowl and in the noon-day heat. That game brought near-disaster and a last-ditch rescue act which kept the Irish on course for a prolonged stay in the States.

The match was staged in temperatures approaching 120 degrees, and this kind of climate suited the Mexicans better than it did the Irish. By this time, Jack Charlton's face was beginning to present a lobster-like redness in appearance, after its exposure to the merciless sun; and *he* wasn't being called upon to run around for 90 minutes, as his players were being asked to do.

To their credit, they ran themselves into the ground in their efforts to counter the Mexicans. But after they had spurned a couple of genuine chances in the first half, they found the opposition coming right back at them and giving even better than they got. Luis Garcia, a forward who played his club football in Spain (with

Atletico Madrid and now with Real Sociedad) caused problems for the Irish defence, and he struck twice to haul his team up the table.

Mexico had been written off by many people, after having lost 1-0 to Norway in their opening match, though that goal had not come until five minutes from time. Now they were in the ascendancy against the Irish, as Luis Garcia scored his first goal with two minutes to go to half-time. A three-man move ended with him hammering a 20-yarder past 'keeper Pat Bonner.

Mid-way through the second period, a squared pass from the left arrived at the feet of Luis Garcia, and once again he made no mistake, to put his team 2-0 ahead. That goal was the signal for Jack Charlton to send on two new faces: Jason McAteer and John Aldridge, although "Aldo" had to wait a while before he was allowed to go on the pitch. That incident on the touchline cost the striker a £1,250 fine, but when he did get into the action, he managed to make an impact as he headed home a precise cross from young McAteer.

However, bookings for Phelan and Irwin meant that the Republic must find two new full-backs for the crunch match against Norway, although Jack Charlton declared himself not too worried about this, since he had various options in defence. What did concern him more was the fact that all four teams in the group were now locked together on three points. Aldridge's goal could turn out to be crucial, dependent upon the way results went in the final group games.

As the Republic's manager summed up, though: "This isn't the end of the world." He knew, however, that his players must claim at least one point from their next match, against Norway in New Jersey, and by now, people were referring to this particular four-team group as the Group of Death. Three countries would go through to the knock-out stages, and one would catch the next plane home.

After the Mexico match, FIFA had come down heavily on the Irish with the £10,000 fines slapped on Jack Charlton and the Football Association of Ireland (plus the £1,250 fine imposed on Aldridge), but apart from the financial penalty there was the added problem for the manager of being banned from the touchline for the game against Norway.

He could talk to his players beforehand, he could talk to them at half-time, but during the action he would have to sit some distance away and communicate by telephone with his second-in-command, Maurice Setters. He admitted later that having to sit and watch was almost more than he could bear, especially during the final few minutes, when to concede a goal would mean that his men must make their exit from the tournament.

But, finally, the whistle blew to signal the end of the match and the Republic's progress into the knock-out stages of the tournament. For once, Norway had come unstuck, and the manner in which they had played left few people lamenting their return home. For the most part, they had seemed content to soak up Irish pressure, without striving too strenuously for victory themselves.

Jack Charlton's verdict: "I'm so proud of the boys - this was a tough group to get through and, at the end of the day, it has been decided on goal difference. On balance, I thought it was a fair result and we deserved to get through. I know, after appearing in the past two finals, that the hardest thing is qualification from the group stages. I'm delighted that we've managed it."

All the countries had finished level on points and on goal difference, but Mexico claimed the top spot, since they had scored most goals, while the Republic, though having an identical record to that of Italy, took second place because they had won the game when the Irish and Italy met in the opening encounter.

At that stage, the Republic looked as if they would be facing Belgium in the knock-out stages, while there remained a chance that Holland, or even Saudi Arabia, would snatch pole position in their group. The Belgians had to play the Saudis, while the Dutch took on Morocco. When the final tally of points and goals was totted up, it turned out that the Republic would be tackling Holland, and not Belgium, who had been the hot favourites to win the group. And it seemed as if this were a favourable omen for the Irish.

When it was realised that the Republic would be in opposition to the Dutch, even some of Holland's own players were expressing their concern at having to face up to Jack Charlton's team . For one thing, Van Basten and Gullit were missing; for another, Ronald Koeman was being rated as past his best; for another, there was talk of dissension inside the Dutch camp; and for yet another thing, some of the Dutch stars admitted that they hadn't been performing well, as a team. They could only hope that things would get better on the night, and they did!

Not that Holland were so superior to the Irish in the opening encounters, but two mistakes in the first half enabled the Dutch to go two goals up, and that proved a task which was too much for the Republic to overcome. It was ironic that Holland, who had scuppered England in Rotterdam and been allowed to recover from a 2-0 deficit at Wembley, should now put paid to the Republic's chances of marching on in the World Cup.

After their promising start, the Republic's players found themselves on the receiving end of some enterprising play from their opponents, and yet it took a lapse by Terry Phelan for the Dutch to make real inroads. It was Dennis Bergkamp who did the damage with the first goal - this was the player who, before the match, had said: "This is not the perfect game for me. I played against the Irish in April and I didn't do well against them. They were so powerful - my one memory was that they seemed to be everywhere." That was then, and this was now, when it really mattered. And Bergkamp came good with his goal.

Four minutes before half-time, the Dutch applied the killer blow. It came from Wim Jonk, and it was a drive delivered at 'keeper Pat Bonner. He moved to make the save, and, to the horror of his team-mates, the ball slipped from his grasp and into the net.

No-one needed to ask what Jack Charlton thought about it all, you could see how he felt, as he half-turned away while making a remark which didn't really need to be translated. Later, he was to say: "We made a couple of basic mistakes, and they cost us the game. Everything went wrong for us; it's hard to get back into a game against Holland after a start like that. I can't ask for more than the lads have given us. I know we have some good players, and I know there are departments where we're a bit short, but nobody can doubt the effort, or the way they tried for us."

The dressing-room scene at half-time scarcely needs to be described: Phelan and Bonner were inconsolable. Big Jack said: "Pat sat with his head in his hands; I didn't have to say anything to him. He knew he'd made a mistake, and the same goes for Terry. That's what can happen in football."

It was Marc Overmars who latched on to Phelan's misplaced header, to set up the chance for Bergkamp to score, and it was a 25-yard drive from Jonk that Bonner (winning his 78th cap - he was already a record-holder) somehow allowed to squirm from his grasp. Bonner was brave enough to appear on TV and tell the world how badly he felt - "desperately sorry for all the fans who have travelled to the United States, as well as for everybody at home. I feel I've let them down, but you don't go out to make mistakes." Of course, you don't.

There was some consolation for Bonner, who had kept out £2M-rated Alan Kelly, whose own father made a club-record total of 447 League appearances for Preston North End and who was a regular for the Republic, too. Pat Bonner learned that Glasgow Celtic's new manager, Tommy Burns, was revoking that free transfer and taking him back to Parkhead, for duty as a player and on the coaching side. So all was not lost, and ambition could still be revived.

Jack Charlton did single out a couple of players as the stars of the Republic show during their World Cup safari. One was Roy Keane, the £3.7M midfielder from Manchester United, and the other was 19-year-old right-back Gary Kelly, of Leeds United. Kelly , who became the youngest player ever to have appeared for the Republic in the finals of the World Cup, had replaced the suspended Denis Irwin, and his overall display made people start to ponder if Irwin could now rely upon being an automatic choice for his native country. Not a bad situation for a manager to be in!

Irwin himself had had a remarkable rise to soccer stardom and, like young Kelly, had kicked off wearing the colours of Leeds United. However, he was then snapped up on a free transfer by Oldham Athletic, who turned him into one of the finest full-backs in English football, and that prompted Manchester United to splash three quarters of a million pounds on him. Like Keane, Irwin went to the World Cup as a winner in both the FA Cup and the Premiership title.

Jack Charlton said of Gary Kelly: "He got off to a rocky start in the opening 10 or 15 minutes (against Holland), but after that he was brilliant. He's going to be some player in the future." Which, of course, prompts the question as to what the future DOES hold, for Big Jack and the Republic of Ireland. So, first, the players.

With the European championships looming in 1996, the Republic is in a group which includes Northern Ireland, Portugal, Austria, Latvia and Lichtenstein. Most of the players who went to the 1994 World Cup will still be around in two years' time; if Alan Kelly has stepped up as first choice for the last line of defence, Pat Bonner might still just be kept in reserve.

Along the back-four line, the Republic can look to Gary Kelly, Denis Irwin, who can play in either full-back position, Terry Phelan, Phil Babb and Alan Kernaghan, and who knows, don't discount Paul McGrath! The odds are, though, that the Republic will have to find another central defender as back-up for Babb and Kernaghan.

In midfield there should still be Andy Townsend and Roy Keane, who is now regarded as the cornerstone of that department. The odds are against Ronnie Whelan and Ray Houghton, but Jason McAteer, of the Liverpool boxing family, looks as if he's arrived to stay. Eddie McGoldrick was 29 when the 1994 World Cup came round, and there must be a question mark against his name with the emergence of McAteer, although there could once again be a place in the squad for him.

When the Republic gained their draw against Northern Ireland at Windsor Park, Belfast, to ensure qualification for the finals, their marksman was Alan McLoughlin, and he now has the best part of two years to switch from a role as "super-sub" to regular. He will still be on the right side of 30 in 1996. And then there is Steve Staunton, who has been an automatic choice, so far.

Like Kevin Moran, who went to the World Cup for the ride, as it turned out, Staunton started out in Gaelic football, and he could have become a star turn in his native land. But instead, he joined Liverpool, won medals, and commanded a £1M fee when he was transferred to Aston Villa. It's a measure of his ability that Liverpool manager Roy Evans had thoughts about trying to sign him back. Still in his mid-20s, Staunton is a left-sided player who can operate with equal effect in midfield, where Jack Charlton played him, or at left-back.

If the Republic face a problem, it seems to be up front, where John Aldridge, Tommy Coyne and Tony Cascarino have all reached a stage of their careers in which international football appears to be figuring less and less on the agenda. Aldridge was 35 when he went to the World Cup, while Cascarino was 31 and so was Coyne. Maybe Coyne will still be around for the European championships, and, barring accidents, David Kelly certainly will be.

Kelly had travelled around a bit in his search for success at League level, but when he went to the finals of the 1994 World Cup he had been capped sixteen times and scored seven goals. At the age of 27, he was by no means over the hill, and perhaps his turn will yet come, as the Republic go for a tilt against England.

One player who, unhappily for him, became almost a forgotten man when the World Cup tournament was staged was Niall Quinn, the lanky striker whose career took off after he joined Manchester City from Arsenal. Quinn, who spent three years as a reserve at Highbury, made such an impact at Maine Road that other clubs had him in their sights, and were prepared to pay almost double the £800,000 which took him to City.

Quinn was to say: "I had three years in World Cup and European-championship squads for the Republic of Ireland, and then went trudging back to the reserves at Arsenal. That was tough to accept, and there were many times when I felt sorry for myself." Now aged 27, Quinn had even more cause to feel sorry for himself when he was stricken down by injury several months before the 1994 World Cup. It was an injury which meant that he could forget all about appearing on the American stage.

By the time he was heading for 100 games with Manchester City, he was also aiming to take his tally of goals to 50, after having knocked in 37 in 88 appearances. And if he gave full credit to Howard Kendall for having signed him, he also paid due tribute to Jack Charlton for having kept him involved at international level, even though this was at a time when he was rated as no more than a reserve-team player at Highbury.

The measure of Quinn's progress at Maine Road could be judged from the fact that as the goals went in, so did the number of inquiries from other clubs increase, and perhaps the most persistent of all the managers who wanted Quinn was Howard Kendall. By that time, he had returned to his first love, Everton, and he was seeking a striker. Quinn was the man he wanted, and he offered well over £1M to City. But to no avail.

Then the beanpole striker suffered a serious knee injury which put him on the sidelines for seven long months. The operation produced a cure, but Quinn had to miss going to the World Cup finals with the Republic of Ireland. It was a devastating blow to the player and to the Republic.

Quinn's first task, of course, as season 1994-95 came around, was to demonstrate that he had regained both fitness and form, and once he shows that he's back to his goal-scoring best, there seems little doubt that he will be pencilled in for European-championship action with the Republic. Ironically, scarcely a week after the final of the 1994 World Cup between Brazil and Italy, Quinn was getting back into the action himself, as he played in a pre-season game for Manchester City.

Quinn was a marksman as he did a 45-minute stint, and he was able to report afterwards that he had felt "not a twinge" while making his comeback. It seems a valid question to ask. Had he been fit to go with the Irish squad to the United states just a few weeks earlier, would the Republic have gone further than they did? Certainly team-mates such as John Aldridge, Tommy Coyne and David Kelly could have fed off him, as he won the aerial duels and knocked the ball down, and, of course, Jack Charlton would also have been looking to the lanky Niall to chip in with a goal or two himself. Quinn's presence could have been priceless.

If the Republic should manage to make progress towards a date with host-nation England in the 1996 European championships, Quinn and Kelly (or Aldridge) could yet turn out to be a good bet as a front-line partnership, and Jack Charlton will surely be keeping a watchful eye on how the three of them fare.

All in all, it doesn't appear as if there will be such a great need for change in the Republic's squad, even if reinforcements are required. There is a solid basis for success, with players of the calibre of Roy Keane, Phil Babb, Jason McAteer, Alan Kernaghan, Steve Staunton, Gary Kelly, Alan Kelly, Terry Phelan, Denis Irwin, Andy Townsend, Niall Quinn and David Kelly. You could form a top-class team from those names alone, and still have a man to spare.

If the days of players such as Paul McGrath, Ray Houghton, Pat Bonner, Kevin Moran, John Aldridge, Tony Cascarino and Ronnie Whelan seemed to be numbered after World Cup '94, there could still be some mileage from the likes of John Sheridan and Eddie McGoldrick along the way, with Houghton and Aldridge each busting a gut to prove that they cannot be discarded lightly.

Sheridan and McGoldrick were both aged 29 when they went to the World Cup, and there was also 27-year-old Alan McLoughlin, who was said to be regarded by Jack Charlton as a kind of super-sub. It was McLoughlin whose late equaliser against Northern Ireland in Belfast clinched the Republic's passage to the States, although he had to play the waiting game when they got there.

When Roy Keane was on his way, he recalled with some wonder just how his career had blossomed: from hopeful trialist with Nottingham Forest to £3.7M man with Manchester United and 22 caps with the Republic of Ireland. At 22, he has 10 years ahead in which to demonstrate that he can be a world-class star.

This one-time-part-time footballer from Cork had just got himself a contract with Forest when the Irish were going to the quarter-finals of the 1990 World Cup, and his day-dream was about breaking into the international arena. One trial game had landed a contract at Forest and, four years on, he was established in his country's side.

Keane certainly suits Big Jack: he's a self-confessed hard-working midfielder who plays within a team pattern. "I don't go off on mazy dribbles. I pass the ball and run to support people." It's a job he does to telling effect, too.

Keane knows what it's like to be tagged the costliest player in English football, even though the fee Manchester United paid for him has been surpassed. Indeed, shortly after the 1994 World Cup, United manager Alex Ferguson himself was musing (and with some concern) on how far transfer fees would escalate, after the £5M barrier had been breached. In Keane's case, there were criticisms (though not from Ferguson) mere months after his arrival at Old Trafford, and the player himself confessed that he was "stunned" to read and hear talk of his being dropped, although he also admitted he hadn't set the world alight.

He stood in awe of some team-mates when he broke through to the international arena and wondered if, indeed, he had any right to be in the squad. But he settled in, collected caps steadily, and can now consider himself not only a regular, but an automatic choice. Whether he will eventually succeed Andy Townsend as the Republic's captain remains to be seen. Keane himself knows he must keep a tight rein on his temperament, yet without quelling that inner fire which makes him want to be a winner, every time out.

When Jack Charlton and his players returned from the United States, Jack himself said he needed time to reflect, he had a bit of thinking to do about his future. Indeed, he had been thinking things over months before he took his team across the Atlantic, as far back, in fact, as the night the Republic met Northern Ireland in their crunch game at Windsor Park. It was a night of decision. And one on which Big Jack proved he was big enough to make a public apology to his Northern Ireland counterpart.

As he walked away after the draw which ensured the Republic's passage to the finals (thanks to the Alan McLoughlin goal which cancelled out the Jimmy Quinn strike which had given Northern Ireland the lead), Jack Charlton made an abusive remark to Billy Bingham who, at 62, was bowing out of the game as a manager. It didn't take Jack long to realise just what he had done, and he was in a hurry to make amends.

Before the teams met, Bingham had had his say and referred to the Republic's players as "mercenaries" - a viewpoint which did not endear him to the opposition. Now Jack Charlton was making his own peace with the Northern Ireland boss in his usual, direct manner.

The scene was the Windsor Park Press room, and as the rival managers prepared to answer questions, Jack Charlton said: "I want to apologise to Billy for what I said at the end of the game. I said a thing I will always regret. I'm very sorry I said it. It was in the heat of the moment. It was out of character."

When asked for his reaction, Bingham declined to elaborate, other than acknowledging: "It was a rude word." He added: "There's no problem , but I take nothing back about mercenaries."

What people did not realise at that time was that Jack Charlton had been on the point of chucking up his job as manager of the Republic. He had spent weeks deliberating what to do, and while he hadn't told his players his thoughts, he had informed his backroom staff. He had told his No.2, Maurice Setters, that if the night went badly in Belfast and the Republic failed to qualify, "I might have to make a decision that wouldn't please my staff."

The decision, of course, could have been a decision to quit. As he said after the Windsor Park game: "Your whole life can change in 12 minutes. If we had failed to qualify, I would have had a chat with the Irish officials to decide whether I stayed on or whether I should step down and leave the job to somebody else for the next competition. I've been thinking over my own future; I've been doing that for weeks."

At the back of Jack's mind was the thought that he might offer his services to England for the 1996 European championships. "If we had gone out I wouldn't have applied for the England job, if it's decided Graham Taylor has to go. But I would have been interested in taking on that role for the European championships, with England as hosts for 1996. Funnily enough, Graham Taylor said to me at the end of the last European-championship qualifying rounds, when they pipped us at the post, 'You'll never beat me, because I'm lucky'. From the moment he said that, he's never had a minute's luck. Things have gone against him."

As he looked ahead to the United States, Charlton also looked to the need for blooding new talent - "You have to pick your best 22 at the time of the finals. The best 22 then may not be the best 22 we have now. We're not loaded down with players. I'd give my right arm for one of the six strikers England have at the moment."

As well as sighing for another top-class striker, Jack Charlton was looking around for a young defender, with the departures of Mick McCarthy, David O'Leary and Kevin Moran, even though he went to the finals as a member of the squad. He came up with Phil Babb and Jason McAteer as a reinforcement for the midfield. Jack likes his little joke. "I need to find a few good players with Irish grannies. We've had eight smashing years and it's still going on, but a lot of the lads who got us this far won't be able to take us any further."

Even then he was rooting for Paul McGrath - "We need him because he is a jewel I would find hard to replace. I'd love to wring another six months out of him. Physically, he's gone back rapidly over the past year, but he's still capable of doing the kind of great job he did against Northern Ireland, and that's what we need in America." That's what he got, too, and maybe Big Jack will manage to "wring" one or two more top-class displays from McGrath before he's finished. He played against Latvia in September 1994.

Jack's thoughts about maybe taking England into the European championships were banished by the Republic's result in Belfast, and he later admitted: "I could never realistically have thought about the England job. If I'd taken it, the Irish would never have forgiven me, and I have too good a relationship with them ever to have upset them."

Now, with the World Cup over, and the European championships to come, the Irish know full well that it's only a matter of time before Big Jack does say farewell. By 1996 he'll be nudging 61, and there's a World Cup in France to come, two years after that. So somewhere on the horizon there has to be a man who can follow in Jack Charlton's footsteps as the team manager of the Republic of Ireland. It's a tall order to ask anyone to fill Big Jack's boots. But someone has to be found.

The Summer of 1994 might have left Charlton musing on where he could dig up a few more "good players with Irish grannies", but the Football Association of Ireland must look even further ahead, to the time Jack Charlton bows out. And there isn't really that long to go.

There may be fleeting thoughts about a former Leeds United team-mate of Jack Charlton's: Johnny Giles, the man Don Revie recommended as his own successor at Elland Road. There may also be some who advocate turning to another one-time gifted midfield player by the name of Liam Brady, whose skills on the park enabled him to play for the likes of Arsenal and in Italy, even if Jack Charlton summarily ended his international career.

Brady, like Giles and Charlton, has been a manager. He tried to revive a sleeping giant in Glasgow Celtic, and after he left Parkhead he wasn't out of a job for long. Brighton persuaded him to become their manager. So Liam Brady would seem an obvious candidate for the job of national team manager.

Then there's a third man: Millwall's Mick McCarthy, who began as an apprentice in his native Barnsley, then was transferred to Manchester City and, like Liam Brady, did a stint with Glasgow Celtic. McCarthy, like Jack Charlton, was a centre-half, and as a manager he went close to taking Millwall to promotion in season 1993-94. As a player, he was in Jack Charlton's international squad at one time, too, and not only is he a Charlton fan, he has been close to Big Jack.

Mick McCarthy could be the man upon whom the mantle falls, once Big Jack makes his exit. If he lands the job, it will be one of the toughest in football, and he knows it. But at least he, or whoever takes up the challenge, can count upon getting some good advice from his predecessor, if, that is, he can manage to collar Big Jack before he's gone fishing.

Postscript

According to report, the man whose name was on everyone's lips was Bob Paisley; he appeared to be the favourite to take charge as manager of the Republic of Ireland's international team. With Liverpool, Bob had won trophies galore before handing over the reins to Joe Fagan, and by 1986 it was the turn of Kenny Dalglish to take the club to fresh honours.

Bob Paisley then was still working in the background at Anfield, but his role did not appear to be anywhere near as prominent as it had been (not that he ever sought the limelight), and it seemed only natural that when others were looking for someone experienced to take charge of their teams, Bob's name should be mentioned.

However, when the 18-man selection committee met to decide upon the name of the man who would guide the Republic of Ireland, hopefully, to success, the Football Association of Ireland came up with another name, that of Jack Charlton. It was said, indeed, that it required a last-minute change of heart by just one member of that 18-strong selection committee for the verdict to be delivered in favour of Big Jack. And so the die was cast.

As one report put it later: "Qualification for a European championship, the final rounds of two World Cups and his own, irascible personality have established him as the most idolised honorary Irishman in history." The report added: "The centre of Dublin came to a standstill when Charlton, 59, born in the pit village of Ashington, Northumberland, joined William Gladstone, George Bernard Shaw, John F Kennedy, Nelson Mandela and Pope John Paul II as a Freeman of the City."

When Big Jack returned from the 1994 World Cup tournament, he did so as a winner, as well as a loser. A winner in the sense not only that he could claim to have the affection of a nation, but that his bank balance had received a healthy boost. It was recorded that "Charlton now enjoys millionaire status."

According to the report, he was paid in the region of £80,000 a year by the Football Association of Ireland for a post he describes as "part-time." He also received a £250,000 bonus for guiding Ireland to the World Cup finals. His popularity in the Emerald Isle has seen him attain cult status.

It was said that Big Jack could earn £3,500 for personal appearances, and that his advisers could accept engagements for every single day of the year, if he wished, but, of course, he didn't. However, he did have "a string of commercial tie-ups". There was the breakfast cereal, the famed Guinness, a certain brand of motor-car and Monaghan Milk, not to mention an Irish bank and an Irish building society. A firm making beds got in on the advertising act, too, while a couple of newspaper columns and a contract with ITV helped to push things along. And who could begrudge him his loot?

While England's Graham Taylor came in for a bitter backlash in the wake of the country's failure to make it to the United States, defeat there for the Republic did nothing to diminish Jack Charlton's popularity, though he insisted he wanted to make certain he remained wanted. "I'll talk to my family and the FAI to get the feel of things. I'm in a position where I have two months before I need to do anything. I'm going to take that time."

In fact, he had made a start, with the European championships in mind, by arranging fixtures, which, of course, would be a considerable help to his successor, should he decide to bow out. One man whose name was being linked with the Irish job after Jack vacated it, Mick McCarthy, offered the opinion: "I don't think we're in the position to name his successor just yet." McCarthy added: "It will be a massive job, after all that Jack has achieved." He could say that again.

Whoever takes over the mantle, there really can never be another Big Jack.

Also available

GEORDIE PASSION
A Lifetime Love of Newcastle United
Mark Hannen

GEORDIE PASSION is a captivating chronicle of Mark Hannen's lifetime devotion to Newcastle United Football Club. From his early childhood in the late 1960s to the present day, it is a story encompassing all the emotions a football fan lives through, from delirious excitement to anger and sorrow, with tales of real life experiences - some humorous, some frightening - thrown in for good measure.

Here are the stars who captivated the huge crowds Newcastle have always attracted: Bobby Moncur, the dour Scotsman, solid as a rock at the heart of the defence; supremely gifted Tony Green, whose promising career was ended prematurely by injury; super star Kevin Keegan, once a player and now Director of football and coaching, who has restored self - belief to United; Beardsley, Waddle and Gascoigne, the local lads made so good; the legendary Supermac, a Geordie hero in the tradition of 'Wor Jackie '; and the sublime Andy Cole, who might just be the best of the lot.

Here too are the great goals, the great games, the great and the not -so -great managers, the magic moments and the all- time lows. Argument will rage over the author's ' best team '; does Supermac deserve to be relegated to the subs' bench in favour of Andy Cole? But all fans will surley agree that beating Sunderland at any time must rate high in the magic moments!

Football, Bill Shankly once remarked, is much more important than either life or death. No Geordie will disagree with that. They are a unique breed and their, and the author's, love of football shines through this delicious diary. **GEORDIE PASSION** is much more than a record of Newcastle's games over twenty- five years. Like Nick Hornby's *Fever Pitch* it is a testimony, written from the heart, to a game that incorporates all of life's emotions in a way no other can.

Hardback; 164 pp with photographs; £9.99

ORDER THESE BOOKS POST & PACKING FREE!

KINNOCK
Dr George Drower
Introduction by the Rt Hon Gerald Kaufman, MP. Special contribution Glenys Kinnock.
Based on interviews with the former Labour Leader and his political friends and enemies, this is a remarkable insight into the character and personality of the man who might have been.
Biography/politics
Hardback; 378pp with photographs; £16.99

A MAN DEPRIVED
Fiszel Lisner and Guy Nathan
Extremely harrowing and moving, this is the story of the man who survived the Nazi death camps for longer than anyone - one week short of five years.
Biography/history
Paperback; 194pp with photographs; £6.99

THE ANGEL WITHIN
Helen Wade
Foreword by The Lord (Brian) Rix CBE. DL.
Humourous and harrowing but ultimately wonderfully uplifting and inspirational, this is the story of the life of a mother of a child with Down's Syndrome.
Biography/sociology
Paperback; 244pp; £6.99

EASTENDERS DON'T CRY
Joe Morgan
Known to his friends as Father Joe and to his enemies as The Godfather, Joe Morgan, former leader of Basildon Council and one of the Labour movement's most active political irritants, tells all in a thoroughly readable account of his life and loves.
Autobiography
Paperback; 180pp; £4.99

THE DEVIL'S DAUGHTER
Christine Hart
Foreword by Colin Wilson.
The incredible story of the girl who came to believe she was the daughter of notorious Moors murderer Ian Brady.
Autobiography
Paperback; 282pp; £5.99

BARCELONA TO BEDLAM
Guy Nathan
Foreword by Reg Drury, former News of the World sports reporter.
Highly topical given Tottenham Hotspur's present predicament, this is the true story of Terry Venables and Alan Sugar and of how a marriage seemingly made in Heaven was consummated in Hell.
Sport/business
Paperback; 382pp; £9.95

GEORDIE PASSION
Mark Hannen

The captivating chronicle of the author's lifetime devotion to Newcastle United Football Club. From his early years in the late 1960s to the present day, this is a testimony, written from the heart, to a game that incorporates all of life's emotions in a way no other can.

Sport

Hardback; 164pp with photographs; £9.99

BIG JACK
Stan Liversedge

The life and times of one of the most widely-respected international football managers who guided Ireland to the 1994 World Cup finals and the sensational victory over Italy. A fascinating and thoroughly enjoyable read.

Sport/biography

Hardback; 172pp with photographs; £9.99

LIVING, LOVING, LEARNING
Clarke Jaggard

Published posthumously, after the author's tragic death in a car accident when he was barely 20, this is a beautiful collection of Clarke Jaggard's poems of love and life and dreams.

Poetry

Paperback; 24pp; £3.95

THE A-Z OF USES FOR AN UNEMPLOYED PERSON
Miles

A sparkling collection of cartoons by the famous ex-cartoonist Miles, who's contribution over many years to several newspapers and publications is expressed in this audaciously funny approach to unemployment.

Humour

Paperback; 28pp; £1.95

These books can be ordered post and packing free. Just send cheque or postal order to the value of the book(s) to:

THE PUBLISHING CORPORATION
Haltgate House
52-54 Hullbridge Road
South Woodham Ferrers
Essex CM3 5NH
Tel/fax: 0245 320462

Please allow 28 days for delivery.